AN
INTRODUCTION
TO
SHARED
INQUIRY

An Introduction to Shared Inquiry

Third Edition

THE GREAT BOOKS FOUNDATION
A nonprofit educational corporation

Text and cover design by William Seabright,
William Seabright & Associates

First Printing
9 8 7 6 5 4
Printed in the United States of America

Published and distributed by

The Great Books Foundation
A nonprofit educational corporation
35 East Wacker Drive, Suite 2300
Chicago, Illinois 60601-2298

CONTENTS

5 Great Books Programs in the Classroom and the Community

Appendix A: Course Materials

Appendix B: Sample Curriculum Units

THE SHARED INQUIRY METHOD OF LEARNING

The goal of Great Books programs is to instill in adults and children the habits of mind that characterize a self-reliant thinker, reader, and learner. Great Books programs are predicated on the idea that everyone can read and understand excellent literature—literature that has the capacity to engage the whole person, the imagination as well as the intellect. As a leader of shared inquiry, you will develop your own mind as you help your participants think for themselves and learn from each other.

Shared inquiry is a distinctive method of learning in which participants search for answers to fundamental questions raised by a text. This search is inherently active; it involves taking what the author has given us and trying to grasp its full meaning, to *interpret* or reach an understanding of the text in light of our experience and using sound reasoning.

The success of shared inquiry depends on a special relationship between the leader and the group. As a shared inquiry leader, you do not impart information or present your own opinions, but guide participants in reaching their own interpretations. You do this by posing thought-provoking questions and by following up purposefully on what participants say. In doing so, you help them develop both the flexibility of mind to consider problems from many angles, and the discipline to analyze ideas critically.

In shared inquiry, participants learn to give full consideration to the ideas of others, to weigh the merits of opposing arguments, and to modify their initial opinions as the evidence demands. They gain experience in communicating complex ideas and in supporting, testing, and expanding their own thoughts. In this way, the shared inquiry method promotes thoughtful dialogue and open debate, preparing its participants to become able, responsible citizens, as well as enthusiastic, lifelong readers.

ABOUT THE BASIC LEADER TRAINING COURSE

The Basic Leader Training Course will prepare you to conduct any of the programs published by the Great Books Foundation—from the Read-Aloud program for prereaders to the Great Books Reading and Discussion Program for adults. In this course you will learn how to identify problems of interpretation, how to formulate questions specific to a reading selection, and how to follow up on your questions to help participants develop their own ideas about outstanding works of literature. This basic process of formulating questions, and striving for answers, is fundamental to all Great Books programs.

Understanding the nature of interpretation and developing the ability to ask meaningful questions is your primary challenge in becoming a Great Books leader. The training course accomplishes this fundamental goal by developing your ability to prepare for and lead Shared Inquiry Discussion—a comprehensive activity that presents the clearest model for the kind of thinking and sharing of ideas that goes on in all Great Books activities.

In the Basic Leader Training Course you will read and discuss selections from a range of Great Books series. Whether you are leading very young students or older ones, all the course readings and activities will help you understand the skills your students will develop throughout the Junior program. Being challenged yourself in the training course—for example, by an advanced reading selection—is essential to learning what it means to be an interpretive reader and an effective model for your students. Discussing a Junior Great Books selection for a young audience, such as "Jack and the Beanstalk," will help you appreciate the depth of ideas that all good literature offers—to adults as well as children.

COURSE REQUIREMENTS

There are two important requirements for your participation in the Basic Leader Training Course. First, you must be committed to leading a Great Books discussion group using the readings published by the Great Books Foundation. For Junior Great Books groups (kindergarten through high school), the administrator responsible must have agreed to purchase the appropriate series of readings or to allow students to purchase their own copies. There is only one exception to the commitment requirement: administrators who will be directly involved in supervising Great Books programs may enroll in the training course, whether or not they plan to lead a group themselves.

Second, you must attend the entire meeting on both days of the course. Each activity in the Basic Leader Training Course is based on activities that precede it, and all work is done in class. Participants who arrive after the course has begun or who miss any other part of it will not be allowed to participate further.

1

BECOMING AN INTERPRETIVE READER

To lead shared inquiry, you must be able to ask questions that guide your participants to find meaning in a text. To do this effectively, you must yourself become an interpretive reader. Being an interpretive reader involves reading actively, raising questions, and striving for understanding. An interpretive reader wants to know why the characters in the story act as they do, what the meaning might be of unusual or surprising events—what an author is trying to communicate through his or her words.

This chapter will take you through the process of interpretive reading—the process that participants in your group will learn with your guidance. As you learn to articulate the problems of meaning that are most important to you, you will become more aware of the depth of insight to be derived from the Great Books selections.

READING ACTIVELY AND TAKING NOTES

Since shared inquiry is a process of raising questions and turning to others for help in finding answers, the first step in leading a group is to discover what you yourself don't understand about the reading selection. Remember that it is the thoughtful questions raised by good interpretive readers that are the focus of Shared Inquiry Discussion as well as the other activities in the Junior Great Books Curriculum. In finding the questions that most interest you,

you will become more familiar with the work as a whole. This, in turn, will enable you to respond more effectively to ideas that members of your group offer—and to see what in the selection is prompting those ideas.

Because Great Books selections are unusually rich in ideas, two readings are necessary. Reading the selection carefully twice and noting your reactions to the work will lead you to think through what the author says and come to terms with the ideas of the selection in your own way. Noting your responses will also help you develop confidence in your understanding of the selection. And by expressing your thoughts—even in scattered marginal comments— you begin to identify those special problems that hold your interest.

On your first reading, concentrate on getting a sense of the work as a whole. When reading fiction, for example, think about what happened in the story, and why. Ask yourself: *Why did the author want to tell this story? How do the characters and events make sense in light of my own experience?*

When reading nonfiction, you might find it easier to follow an author's argument if you pencil in your own titles for sections, paragraphs, and pages. You might also outline a selection, numbering its major points and noting supporting statements and examples. Rough diagrams or charts can sometimes help you make sense of complex passages. If you find a section of the text particularly difficult, try putting the author's argument into your own words. In addition, note any term that the author seems to use in a special way and trace it throughout the work to understand what it means in different contexts.

Give yourself some time between readings to let your ideas and impressions settle. On your second reading, you may want to concentrate on specific portions of the selection that interest or puzzle you, analyzing them and relating them to the work as a whole. Because you already know the outcome of the story or understand the general thrust of the author's argument, you can more clearly recognize the connections among incidents in the plot or points in the argument. Having the author's "big picture" in mind as you read will also make unusual word choice and recurrent ideas and images more noticeable. Your second reading will let you refine and correct first impressions, answer many of your initial questions, and find some new problems of meaning.

Following are a few note-taking suggestions.

Note anything you do not understand. If a character says or does something that puzzles you, note it in the margin. If you find some aspect of an author's argument unclear, make a note of what perplexes you.

Note anything you think is especially important. Look for those passages that strike you as particularly significant. Try to express exactly why they attract your attention and hold your interest. If you have a question about an essential part of an author's argument, write it in the margin. Note also the connections you perceive between different parts of the selection. If you begin to see a pattern in the author's use of language or in a character's actions, make a note to remind yourself to look again at related passages.

Note anything about which you feel strongly. If you disagree with an author's argument, make a note about why you differ. If a character's actions trouble you, explain your response in the margin. Noting your agreement can be equally useful. Passages that cause you to respond strongly, either positively or negatively, will usually provoke a similar reaction in others, and might therefore contain a problem on which to focus in discussion.

Some leaders find it helpful to distinguish the notes from their first and second readings. They use different colored pens or different markings, or switch from pen to pencil. The next page shows the notes a reader took on the beginning of "Jack and the Beanstalk"; the gray notes are from the second reading.

JACK AND THE BEANSTALK

English folktale as told by Joseph Jacobs

There was once upon a time a poor widow *[why?]* who had an only son named Jack and a cow named Milky-white. And all they had to live on was the milk the cow gave every morning, which they carried to the market and sold. But one morning Milky-white gave no milk and they didn't know what to do. *[desperate situation]*

"What shall we do, what shall we do?" said the widow, wringing her hands.

"Cheer up, mother, I'll go and get work *[Naive? Optimistic?]* somewhere," said Jack.

"We've tried that before, and nobody would take you," said his mother. "We must *[why not?]* sell Milky-white and with the money start a shop or something."

"All right, mother," says Jack. "It's market day today, and I'll soon sell Milky-white, and then we'll see what we can do."

So he took the cow's halter in his hand, and off he started. He hadn't gone far when he met a funny-looking old man who said to him: "Good morning, Jack."

"Good morning to you," said Jack, and wondered how he knew his name. *[Cautious?]*

"Well, Jack, and where are you off to?" said the man.

"I'm going to market to sell our cow here."

"Oh, you look the proper sort of chap to sell cows," said the man. "I wonder if *[flattery]* you know how many beans make five."

"Two in each hand and one in your mouth," says Jack, as sharp as a needle. *[Is this silly or clever?]* *[? Odd!]*

"Right you are," says the man. "And here they are, the very beans themselves," he went on, pulling out of his pocket a number of strange-looking beans. "As you *[Sarcasm? or praise?]* are so sharp," says he, "I don't mind doing a swap with you—your cow for these beans."

"Go along," says Jack. "Wouldn't you *[Helping or taking advantage?]* like it?"

"Ah! you don't know what these beans are," said the man. "If you plant them overnight, by morning they grow right up to the sky."

"Really?" says Jack. "You don't say so."

"Yes, that is so, and if it doesn't turn out to be true you can have your cow back." *[Guarantee!?]*

"Right," says Jack, and hands him over Milky-white's halter and pockets the beans. *[What makes him decide? Smart? Or Foolish?]*

Back goes Jack home, and as he hadn't gone very far it wasn't dusk by the time he got to his door.

"Back already, Jack?" said his mother. "I see you haven't got Milky-white, so you've sold her. How much did you get for her?"

"You'll never guess, mother," says Jack.

"No, you don't say so. Good boy! Five pounds, ten, fifteen, no, it can't be twenty."

"I told you you couldn't guess. What do you say to these beans; they're magical, *[man never said this]* plant them overnight and—"

"What!" says Jack's mother. "Have you been such a fool, such a dolt, such an idiot, as to give away my Milky-white, the best milker in the parish, and prime beef to boot, *[cruel]* for a set of paltry beans? Take that! Take that! Take that! And as for your precious beans, here they go out of the window. And *[She plants beans]* now off with you to bed. Not a sip shall you drink, and not a bit shall you swallow this very night."

One note from the first reading poses a question about something not understood: "Why does Jack decide to trade the cow for the beans?" Other notes express emotional responses ("cruel mother"); offer judgments about characters' words and actions ("optimistic," "naive," "flattery"); or indicate observations about things that seem important ("The man never exactly tells Jack the beans are magical" and "The mother actually plants the beans").

On the second reading, new responses are noted: "Is Jack's answer to the man a silly or a clever one?" and "What good is the guarantee?" Earlier notes are reconsidered and some guesses are made about their meaning: "Is the man flattering Jack in order to take advantage of him?" and "Was it clever of Jack to trade the cow for five beans? Or was he just lucky that things turned out so well?" Some details not noted before are now seen as important: "Is 'sharp as a needle' praise or sarcasm?" and "Why does the author make the mother a widow?"

Looking for genuine problems of meaning in the selection, those that persist as problems even after careful reflection, is one of the aims of active, interpretive reading. But often, especially at this stage, you cannot be sure if something is truly problematic or if it can be easily resolved with a little more thought. For this reason, you should be open-minded and jot down any reactions you have. Be alert to all the possibilities of meaning you see in the selection, and don't be overly concerned with assessing your responses.

DISCOVERING YOUR OWN INTERPRETIVE QUESTIONS

After carefully reading a complex story or essay, you will probably have many questions about why things happened the way they do, or what the author is trying to communicate. In shared inquiry we distinguish three kinds of questions you might ask about a work.

Questions of Fact, Interpretation, and Evaluation

When reading and experiencing a work of literature, we do so on three levels. The first and most fundamental level is that of fact, all the "givens" of a work. In fiction, any information the author provides about the world of the story—every detail of setting, character, and plot—is a "fact," whether or not it corresponds to our perception of reality. For example, in "Jack and the Beanstalk," it is a "fact" that ogres live in the sky. In nonfiction, the author's statements—propositions, lines of argument, conclusions—are "facts." Comprehension and appreciation of the facts of a work lay the foundation for the next level of reading: interpretation.

To interpret a story or essay is to construct explanations of what the author wants us to think about and experience through his or her words. Interpretation begins with the questions that come to us as we read. Why does a character act in a certain way? Why does the author include a particular detail? Why do things turn out as they do? What does a certain word mean in context? As we develop answers to such questions, we get a better sense of how the parts of the work fit together and of what the work means.

The third way we respond to a work of literature is evaluation. When we evaluate a work, we consider its bearing on our lives and its broader implications, even if it poses ideas that seem inconsistent with our own values and personal experience. We judge what the author has written, deciding for ourselves whether it is true. Just as a firm grasp of the facts of a work is essential to thoughtful interpretation, a solid understanding of the author's meaning is the basis for intelligent evaluation.

Corresponding to these three levels of reading are three kinds of questions that are addressed in shared inquiry: questions of fact, interpretation, and evaluation. A **question of fact** has only one correct answer. It asks participants to recall something the author says, and can usually be answered by pointing to a passage in the selection. For example, the answer to the question *What does Jack take from the ogre the first time he goes up the beanstalk?* is explicitly stated in the text: a bag of gold.

Sometimes, however, a question of fact cannot be answered by pointing to any single place in the text; rather, its answer must be inferred from other facts available in the selection. For instance, the answer to the question *Does Jack plan to steal from the ogre when he climbs the beanstalk for the first time?* does not appear explicitly in the story. But we can conclude that since this was Jack's first climb (a fact), he could not have had knowledge of the ogre and so could not have planned to steal from him (reasonable inference). Since this inference represents the only logical conclusion, we consider it a "fact" of the story. The question *Does the golden harp want to go with Jack?* is also factual for the same reason: although the answer does not appear explicitly in the text, it can be inferred with reasonable certainty from other evidence that *is* explicit. The fact that the harp cries out for its master is sufficient proof that it does not want to go with Jack.

A **question of interpretation** asks participants to look carefully at what happens in a story and to consider what the story means. Unlike a factual question, an interpretive question has more than one reasonable answer that can be supported with evidence from the text. For example, consider the question *Why does Jack make the third trip to the ogre's house?* Several answers are possible. Jack may have been driven by curiosity or by greed to see what else the ogre had in his house. Perhaps he longed for further adventures, or took pleasure in outwitting the ogre. Or Jack may have wanted to prove himself to his mother, or been worried that the hen might stop laying, just as Milky-white had gone dry. The text provides reasonable support for each of these answers. Because the question raises a substantial problem of meaning, and can be answered in more than one way based on evidence in the story, it is capable of sustaining a rewarding discussion.

Questions of evaluation ask us to think about something in the work in light of our own knowledge, values, or experience of life, to decide whether we agree with the author's ideas or point of view. Consider this example of an evaluative question: *Is it necessary to take risks—as Jack does—in order to grow up and be responsible?* Participants will be prepared to address the broad issues in this question only after coming to their own understanding of how Jack behaves and matures throughout the story. If such questions are introduced prematurely, before the meaning of the work has been fully explored, they tend to invite digression and discussion of matters having little to do with the selection itself.

The distinguishing characteristics of factual, interpretive, and evaluative questions are summarized below:

A **factual question** has only one correct answer.

An **interpretive question** has more than one answer that can be supported with evidence from the text.

An **evaluative question** asks us to decide whether we agree with the author's ideas or point of view. The answer to an evaluative question depends on our own knowledge, experience, and values, as well as on our own interpretation of the work.

To put it another way: Questions of fact ask, "What does the author say?" Questions of interpretation ask, "What does the author mean by what he or she says?" Questions of evaluation ask, in light of your interpretation, "Do I agree with what the author is saying?"

In shared inquiry, we concentrate on questions of interpretation, referring to the facts of the work for evidence and reserving evaluation for the time when our interpretation is complete.

Developing Interpretive Questions from Your Notes

Reviewing your notes is an excellent way to develop interpretive questions. As you look back over the work, think again about why you noted particular passages and write down your ideas in the form of questions. Some of the notations you made may no longer seem significant, but others will suggest ideas that continue to hold your interest.

Many experienced leaders will write twenty or more questions as they consider and reconsider the problems of meaning in a selection. Notes which focus on the following are especially good sources for interpretive questions.

Character motivation. Look for notes that question the reasons behind a character's statements, actions, or thoughts. For example, you might be curious about why the ogre's wife seems to betray her husband by helping Jack. This might lead you to ask, *Why does the ogre's wife want to keep Jack from being eaten?* Is she impressed with Jack's bravery? His politeness? Or is she moved by how hungry and desperate Jack sounds?

Striking or unusual use of language. You might be surprised at the way an author expresses an idea or casts a description. For example, thinking about Jack's reply to the funny-looking old man might lead you to ask this question: *Why does Jack answer the old man's question by saying, "Two in each hand and one in your mouth"?* Does Jack's answer indicate that he is worried about the future, and where his next meal is coming from? Does his answer suggest immaturity—or a quick wit?

Prominent details. Although you won't want to question the purpose of every detail, some details can function as important elements in an interpretation. Consider the question *Why does the author make Jack's mother a poor widow?* Does it seem significant to you that Jack is poor and fatherless? What bearing does this information have on our understanding of Jack's adventures? Expressing your question about how to interpret a detail you noted can lead your group to a fresh understanding of a story or essay.

Words or phrases that can be understood in more than one way. Often, the way a word or phrase is used will attract your attention and cause you to consider whether it has special significance. If examining the context of the word or phrase doesn't help you pinpoint a definite interpretation—and, in the case of a striking word, if a dictionary does not seem to settle the matter— then write a question that calls attention to the ambiguity you find. For example, the author writes that even after his second trip up the beanstalk, Jack was "not content." But why does Jack feel this way? Does he want more gold—or does he long for further adventures? Your curiosity about Jack's feelings could lead to the interpretive question *Why isn't Jack content even though he has riches to last a lifetime?*

Connections between passages, characters, incidents, or ideas. The various parts of a well-crafted work of literature are interconnected; they support one another. Discovering the meaning of a story or essay depends on understanding the relationships between its parts. In "Jack and the Beanstalk," Jack's three adventures in the sky are similar in many respects— the climb, the theft, the escape—but their parallelism also serves to highlight significant differences. Noting that on his second trip Jack confronts the ogre's wife in a more assured manner, you could ask, *Why is Jack so much bolder in asking the ogre's wife for food on his second trip than on his first?* Is he just hungry, as he was before? Is he gaining time to look around? Is he braver—or is he being foolhardy? In this case, comparing parallel scenes can spotlight Jack's developing confidence and cleverness as well as the wife's changing role. Other examples are *Why does the author have the ogre's wife act more kindly to Jack than his own mother?* or *Why does the author have Jack take a bag of gold, a magic hen, and a golden harp in that order?*

But the most important source of interpretive questions is your thoughtful consideration of what the entire work seems to mean. After reading a selection the second time, go over passages that seem especially significant or striking, such as those dealing with a moment of crisis or a decisive change in a character. Then step back and ask yourself what, in broad terms, are the work's major themes and ideas. For instance, thinking about the changes Jack undergoes in the course of his adventures could lead you to ask, *Why do Jack's adventures enable him to grow up successfully in the story?* Often, considering a more comprehensive problem of meaning will change the focus of other questions and bring new interpretive issues to mind.

2

BECOMING A SHARED INQUIRY LEADER: TURNING TO OTHERS WITH YOUR QUESTIONS

Throughout shared inquiry, the leader provides guidance only by careful questioning. Because the leader does not provide answers, participants are challenged to think for themselves. By trying out ideas and exchanging and examining opinions, they build their own answers to interpretive questions and develop their own ways of understanding the selection.

If you are conducting the full Junior Great Books Curriculum, you will see ideas develop at many stages in the reading process. But Shared Inquiry Discussion—in which you turn to your participants for help in exploring your interpretive questions—is the best model for seeing how leaders work with the ideas of their participants and learn from them.

Shared Inquiry Discussion is an opportunity, after participants have read the selection twice and gained a sense of its interpretive issues, to explore an important interpretive question in depth. Discussion begins when the leader poses a prepared interpretive question to which he or she does not yet have a satisfactory answer. As participants respond, the leader follows up on their ideas, asking questions about how the responses relate to the interpretive question and to other ideas put forward by the group and about how they are supported by and illuminate the text. Each participant brings a unique perspective that influences how he or she understands the assigned story or essay. By sharing their interpretations, participants discover new aspects of the work and can deepen or even change their initial understanding of it.

PREPARING TO LEAD SHARED INQUIRY DISCUSSION

Leading shared inquiry calls for a balance between planning and spontaneity. As you prepare, you want to become familiar enough with a selection that you will be able to respond helpfully to your participants' ideas and insights. You also want to know the work well enough to be able to guide your participants to passages in the text that are relevant to their ideas—and to your questions.

The best way to achieve this "planned spontaneity" is to keep an open mind about a selection and write your own questions. The process of writing—and improving—your questions will lead you to grapple with, and form preliminary ideas about, a work's most important interpretive problems. You should write down any questions that occur to you during your reading or that you have developed from your notes, without critically evaluating them. As you prepare, you will be able to discard any of your initial questions that turn out to be less interesting or significant. Others you will revise and improve. Your goal is to compile a list of questions that are especially thought-provoking and important.

Choosing a Question to Lead in Discussion: What Makes a Good Interpretive Question?

Shared inquiry should be a process of discovery for both you and your participants. When you ask a question to start discussion, in effect you are saying, "Here is a place in the text that suggests something important to me, but I'm having trouble deciding what it means. With your help, I would like to think more about this problem." You want your participants to be able to respond—and to want to respond—when they hear your initial question. You want them to understand right away what you are asking and to be able to think about what details in the selection bear on the problem you have raised.

What makes a good interpretive question, one that can get your participants interested immediately?

You should have genuine doubt about the answer or answers to the question. Doubt means that after identifying and considering a problem of meaning, you are still unsure about how best to resolve it. The problem persists, and so you want to share the question with your group to find out what they think about it.

To be sure that you have doubt about a question, try to write at least two different answers and support each with evidence from the selection. If the text seems to provide reasonable support for at least two answers, and you're not sure which you prefer, then for you that question raises a point about which you have doubt. It would be difficult to have doubt about the answer to *Is Scho as good a ball player as Glennie and Monk?* because the text plainly indicates that the answer is "no." Likewise, *Do Monk and Glennie try to exclude Scho from their game?* is not suitable for Shared Inquiry Discussion because it has only one reasonable answer based on the evidence in the story.

Doubt does not mean, "I know the best answer, but my participants may not." Questions meant to lead your participants to a single answer or to an insight that you think is important are not suitable for shared inquiry because such questions do not help participants work with and develop their own ideas. Be aware of how a question—by its wording or assumptions—may imply a predetermined answer. For example, the question *Don't you think the title "A Game of Catch" refers to more than Monk and Glennie's game?* tends to push participants to respond with a "yes." Similarly, *Do you really think Scho fell from the tree accidentally?* seems with the term "really" to betray the leader's lack of doubt about the answer.

You should care about the question. Write questions about interpretive problems that truly interest you; concentrate on problems that you feel are important. Your enthusiasm for a question can be contagious, leading to a lively exchange of ideas among the members of your group. If you ask a question you don't care about, your participants will sense your lack of interest and respond superficially with whatever they imagine will quickly bring discussion to a close.

Your question should be discussible. Does the question send you to the selection for answers? And does the selection contain the evidence needed to support answers? Sometimes, a work captures us so thoroughly we lose track of the limits of the world that the author has created. The question *How will Glennie and Monk react the next time they are playing catch and Scho comes along?* inquires about a period of time not encompassed by the selection, and so involves speculating beyond the facts of the story. Also speculative are questions that ask what would have happened had events in the work been different, as in the example: *How might the story have turned out if Glennie and Monk hadn't made Scho wait so long?* Finally, some questions about specific details, such as *Do you think maybe Scho can't afford a glove? What grade is Scho in?* or *What do you imagine Scho's home life is like?* are not discussible because answers cannot be supported with evidence from the text. Unlike a good interpretive question, these questions will all fail to keep participants grounded in the text and moving toward a fuller understanding of the story.

Your question should be clear. An interpretive question should be easy for your participants to understand; otherwise, they will have to spend valuable discussion time simply trying to figure out what the question means. Consider how your participants would respond to the unnecessarily difficult language of this question: *Does Scho exhibit symptoms of delusion in his verbal attempts to control Glennie and Monk?* A question that is poorly focused will also seem unclear: *Why does the author have Scho climb up to what he calls a "wonderful seat," and which the author later calls a "cradle of slight branches"?* Both of these questions would stump most participants. In writing questions, strive for a clarity and sharpness that will prompt your group to begin thinking of answers right away.

Your question should be specific to the selection. If a question can be applied to many other selections with only a few word changes, it is probably too general. *How are Monk and Glennie alike and unlike? What is the main idea of the story?* are examples of overly broad questions that could easily be altered for use with other stories. Such questions do not give participants a definite problem to explore; nor will they spark the interest of your group. To bring the problem you want to consider into focus and to avoid getting vague responses, make your questions as specific to the selection as you can.

Improving Your Questions

Many of the questions you write after your second reading of the selection will need to be reworked or revised before discussion. Some will turn out to be factual, evaluative, not fully developed, or unclear. Or you may find that several weaker questions can evolve into a single one that better expresses a particular problem. Sometimes, you'll write several versions of the same question. Deciding which formulation of a question is best involves your estimation of what will get your participants to react. While there are no rules for transforming your initial questions into interpretive questions that are sharply focused and provocative, the following suggestions will help you revise your questions.

Revise questions that have only one answer. If a question turns out to be factual, or if you eventually come to lack doubt about it, check to see if its answer will lead you to an interpretive question. For example, your initial thinking about "A Game of Catch" might lead you to ask, *Does Scho play a game of his own?* The answer to this question—that Scho does indeed play his own game in pretending to control Glennie and Monk—suggests the interpretive question *Why does Scho play a game in which he pretends to control Glennie and Monk?* This revision, unlike the original, has a number of different answers because it explores Scho's motives.

If you come to lack doubt about the answer to a question, try revising it to include a reasonable assumption. Suppose that in thinking about the question *Does Scho remain an outsider throughout the story?* you eventually conclude that for you the answer is "yes." Instead of discarding the question, change its focus by making use of your assumption that Scho remains an outsider: *Why does Scho remain an outsider throughout the story?* Other examples of questions that incorporate assumptions are: *Why does Scho feel more powerful in the tree than he does on the ground? Why does Scho deliberately fall from the tree?* If the assumption is shared by everyone, it serves as an appropriate point for the discussion to begin.

If participants challenge your assumption—if, for instance, someone doubts that Scho felt more powerful in the tree, or that he fell on purpose—then opposing viewpoints will be discussed and weighed against the evidence in the text.

Revise evaluative questions. If a question on your list is evaluative—*Is Scho wrong to interfere with Glennie and Monk's game?*—try rewording it so that instead of calling for a judgment it asks about a problem of meaning in the text, such as *Why does Scho interfere with Glennie and Monk's game?* The former question asks that participants judge Scho's behavior; the revision encourages them to discuss Scho's motivation using evidence from the story. Similarly, *How could Monk and Glennie have been nicer to Scho?* would probably lead to pious moralizing, rather than to a deeper understanding of the story.

Clarify your wording. Some questions might be hard for your group to answer because of difficult vocabulary or jargon. The question *Is it ego gratification that makes Scho play his game?* assumes that your participants have a knowledge of psychological terminology. But the revision *Why does Scho pretend he can control Glennie and Monk?* addresses the problem of Scho's motivation in more direct terms suggested by the text.

Sometimes, familiar but abstract words like "good" or "evil" can also make your question unclear. The question *Are we to conclude that Scho is evil at heart?* could result in a semantic tug-of-war between participants who have different ideas of what "evil at heart" means. If this occurs, be prepared to direct your participants to a specific incident in the text that made you think of the problem in the first place. Ask, for instance, *Why does Scho continue to taunt Glennie and Monk even after they invite him to come down and play catch?*

Avoid literary terminology. Questions that use or ask about literary terms suggest that participants need a particular vocabulary to appreciate good literature, and that discussion is merely a technique for teaching them. Questions such as *Is Scho a tragic hero? How does the author foreshadow Scho's unhappy end? Is "A Game of Catch" an allegory of the fall of man? Are there any important symbols in the story?* can inhibit a free exchange of ideas by making participants feel that they are being tested in discussion. Moreover, it is quite difficult to maintain your own doubt about the answers to such questions. General questions about what something "represents" or "symbolizes" should be revised. Instead of *Is Scho's falling from the tree symbolic?*, ask more specific questions such as *Why does the author have Scho play his game in a tree?* or *Why does the author have Scho fall from the tree?*

Make vague questions specific. The question *What is Scho's attitude toward Monk and Glennie?* might not give participants enough information about the problem you want them to consider. Scho's attitude toward the boys, which changes in the course of the story, would be better explored through more specific questions, such as *Why does Scho say he can make Glennie and Monk do whatever he wants?* and *Why doesn't Scho accept Glennie's invitation to come down from the tree and play catch?*

Present distinct alternatives, where possible. Be alert to interpretive problems that require a choice between two plausible answers that are in especially strong opposition. If you have genuine doubt about which of the answers is preferable, then instead of leaving the question open, state the alternatives for your participants to weigh. For example, the question *Why does Glennie ask Scho if he has his glove, when it's obvious that he doesn't?* could be revised this way: *Is Glennie's question "Got your glove?" an invitation for Scho to play, or a way of getting rid of him?* Such a question can make discussion more interesting because participants will have to take a stand

and choose between competing points of view. Be certain, though, that the alternatives you offer in the question are the ones most strongly suggested by the selection. If several other answers are equally plausible, your question could restrict inquiry.

not so, neither is an option

Rethink questions that include the author. Some of your questions will ask about the author's attitude toward the characters, reasons for including specific details, or purpose in writing the story. In reviewing such questions, consider whether you should shift the focus from the author to the characters. For example, the question *Why does the author have Scho continue his game after Monk apologizes to him?* will force your group to think about Scho from an unnecessarily distant perspective. By asking instead, *Why does Scho continue his game after Monk apologizes to him?*, you will get your participants to explore Scho's motives and feelings more directly.

On the other hand, the question *Why are Glennie and Monk so good at their game?* is less suited for shared inquiry than *Why does the author make Glennie and Monk so good at their game?* The first question would elicit only speculative answers—perhaps the boys were naturally athletic or played together often—which would not lead participants to a greater understanding of the story. The second question, however, raises the larger—and more discussible—matter of why Glennie and Monk's skill is important to the story.

Many interpretive issues can be phrased as either a problem of character motivation or a problem of the author's intention. However, the addition of "the author" to a question like *Why does Scho climb the tree?* will alter the type of answers you hear in discussion. Do you want your participants to talk about Scho's reasons for climbing the tree—or the author's reasons for having him do it? In a case like this, be sure to use the form of the question that reflects the problem you want to explore with your group.

Improving interpretive questions is not a science. The phrasing you choose represents your best judgment about what will most clearly convey an interpretive problem as you see it and what will most effectively get your participants involved. Consider the following variations on the question, *Why does Scho play a game in which he pretends to control Glennie and Monk?*, which appears in the Teacher's Edition for Junior Great Books Series Five, Second Semester:

> *Why does Scho pretend he controls Glennie and Monk?*
>
> *Does Scho pretend he controls Glennie and Monk because he wants to disrupt their game or because he wants to be included?*
>
> *Why does Scho play a game that disrupts Glennie and Monk's game of catch?*
>
> *Does Scho disrupt Glennie and Monk's game out of spite or because he wants to be noticed?*

Although each of these questions has a slightly different focus, they all concern Scho's motivation for playing his game—and they would all be suitable for Shared Inquiry Discussion. When improving your interpretive questions, keep in mind that there is no such thing as the "perfect" wording. Refining ideas—including your own—is part of the process of shared inquiry. In discussion, you should be flexible about your questions and be ready to rephrase them if your participants need help in responding.

Preparing Basic Questions and Clusters

After writing and revising your interpretive questions, you need to think about how you will be using them in discussion. Which questions address major problems and themes? Which probe more specific details? What are the relationships among the questions? To get a handle on the relative importance of each question, and to put into sharper perspective the larger, more comprehensive problems of meaning suggested by the work, you should group your questions into clusters.

Grouping your interpretive questions involves putting together those questions that bear on the same problem of interpretation and then identifying—or writing—a basic question for each group. A **basic question** is one that addresses in a comprehensive way a central problem of meaning in the selection; answering a basic question satisfactorily requires the examination of many passages in the text. A **cluster** is a group of interpretive questions that are all related to a single basic question. The questions in a cluster might approach the problem in the basic question from different perspectives, address separate parts of the problem, or examine various passages that bear on the problem.

Working on "A Game of Catch," a leader might develop a cluster that looks something like this:

> Basic Question: *Is the story suggesting that Glennie and Monk treat Scho unfairly?*
>
> *Is Glennie's question "Got your glove?" an invitation for Scho to play, or a way of getting rid him?*
>
> *Why does Glennie invite Scho down from the tree to play catch?*
>
> *Why does Monk apologize for causing Scho's fall from the tree?*
>
> *Why does Monk begin to throw the ball to Glennie once or twice before he gives Scho the hard, bumpy grounder?*

The basic question, which looks into the behavior of Glennie and Monk with respect to Scho, addresses a central problem of understanding the way the characters interact. Each question in the cluster refers to a point in the story when the motives of Glennie or Monk are in doubt: Glennie's ambiguous question, "Got your glove?"; his suggestion that Scho climb down from the tree; Monk's apology; and his hard throw to Scho. These questions thus direct attention to passages containing evidence relevant to answering the basic question.

In Shared Inquiry Discussion, asking a number of related questions—rather than an assortment of unrelated ones—will make your group's exploration of the selection more thorough and coherent. But a cluster is only a provisional plan for helping your participants resolve the comprehensive interpretive problem posed by your basic question. Discussion itself will determine which questions from the cluster you'll use, and when to use them.

Here's how to prepare clusters from your list of interpretive questions:

1. *Group your questions, placing together those that seem to deal with the same problem of meaning.* When you are finished, you should have three or four groups, each containing several questions that concern an interpretive problem you wish to explore. To test whether a question belongs in a given cluster, begin to answer it; the answers you get will help you determine if the question is related to others in the group. Some questions will not seem to fit with any of the others; put these aside.

2. *Select or write a basic interpretive question for each cluster.* Examine each group to determine whether it contains a question that states the problem in a comprehensive fashion. If no question in the group seems "basic," write an interpretive question to cover the main issue the cluster addresses.

3. *Develop the clusters.* Consider whether any of the questions you have set aside can be revised and included in a cluster. (If not, consider whether one or more of these questions can form the beginning of another group.) Write additional questions to fill out the clusters as necessary; you should have four or five questions in each cluster. Check to see whether the answers to each question in a cluster will help you

answer the basic question. If two questions bring up similar answers, discard the question that seems less clear. If a question is only a close restatement of the basic question, drop it or revise it.

4. *Arrange the questions in each cluster in an order that makes sense to you.*

After working with your questions and grouping them, you will find that some of your clusters address problems that seem more comprehensive, more essential to the meaning of the work, or just more interesting to you. Select one of these clusters for your group to discuss first. It is the basic question from this cluster that you will use to initiate Shared Inquiry Discussion. Keep the other clusters on hand; having basic questions in reserve will let you go on to a new problem after your initial one has been satisfactorily explored.

LEADING SHARED INQUIRY DISCUSSION

Shared Inquiry Discussion begins when you ask your group a basic question that will serve as the focus. As leader, your aim is to elicit your participants' ideas and opinions about your basic question. You want to help them share, test, and clarify their thinking and, ultimately, to resolve for themselves the problem of meaning you have posed. You do all this by asking **follow-up questions.** A few of your follow-up questions will come from the clusters of interpretive questions you wrote during your preparation, but most will be your spontaneous responses to your participants' comments. Follow-up questions will allow you to clarify responses, to ask for evidence in support of opinions, to pursue intriguing lines of inquiry, and to invite new responses to your initial question.

The Four Rules of Discussion

During discussion, participants exchange their ideas freely, but within the framework of four rules that make Shared Inquiry Discussion a disciplined activity.

1. *Only those who have read the selection may take part in discussion.* Participants who have not either read the selection or had it read aloud to them cannot contribute intelligently to a discussion of its meaning. Since they cannot support their opinions with evidence from the selection, or bring a knowledge of the text to bear on the opinions of others, they will only confuse and distract other members of the group.

2. *Discussion should focus only on interpreting the assigned story or essay.* Talking at length about participants' personal experiences or values, or their opinions about other books or movies, is not relevant to the interpretation of the text, and may exclude other members of the group from discussion.

3. *Do not introduce outside opinions unless you can back them up with evidence of your own.* In Shared Inquiry Discussion participants share ideas, but each individual must think for himself or herself. If participants rely on the opinions of others—a spouse or parents, a textbook or an encyclopedia—they will not develop their own ideas and insights, or become active, interpretive readers.

4. *Leaders may only ask questions; they may not answer them.* Your job as leader is to help yourself and your participants understand a selection by asking questions that prompt thoughtful inquiry. If participants get the impression that you have "the" correct answer, they will look for you to supply it instead of developing their own interpretations.

Observing the four rules of Shared Inquiry Discussion helps you and your participants make the best possible use of your discussion time. Rule 1 ensures that participants discuss and hear informed opinions about the reading under discussion. Rules 2 and 3 reinforce participants' comprehension and recall of the selection and set the standard for how opinions are weighed. They also encourage participants to think independently. Rule 4 gives participants the responsibility for developing and expressing their own ideas. By exercising this responsibility together with the other members of the group, participants learn to value their own thinking and to respect the opinions of others.

Beginning the Discussion

For your Great Books discussions, try to arrange the room so that everyone can sit in a circle or square. This type of arrangement stimulates discussion by making it possible for all members of the group to listen and talk directly to one another. It also helps reinforce the idea that your role in shared inquiry is that of a partner, and shows students that the ideas of their fellow participants will be a major source of help in gaining insight into a selection. If your group is large—thirty or more—assign participants to smaller groups of ten to twenty for discussion, so that each student can receive more attention and have several opportunities to speak. (Students not engaged in discussion can read independently.) Be sure your participants have a convenient surface where they can put their books down, open them up, and refer to them regularly. Discussion is very much an "open book" activity.

Making Up a Seating Chart

A seating chart is an extremely useful tool for keeping track of participants' ideas and comments during discussion. Once everyone is seated, make up a seating chart and write your question at the top of the chart.

During discussion, you will jot down participants' comments next to their names. Keep your notations short; all you usually need is a word or phrase to indicate important ideas. Lines drawn between names can highlight opinions that agree or conflict. Although writing down participants' ideas may take some time, slowing the pace of discussion is often desirable. It gives participants a chance to think about their answers and make connections between related ideas, and it gives you time to think of follow-up questions that make use of your group's comments.

Here is what a seating chart might look like in the middle of a discussion of the basic question *Why does Jack climb the beanstalk the third time?*

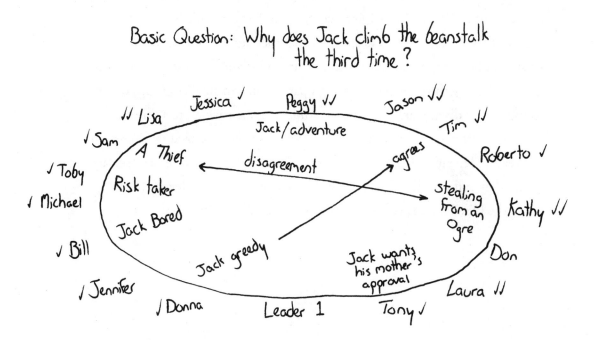

Using a seating chart during discussion will encourage you to call on each participant. Preface each of your questions with the participant's name to give him or her time to focus on your question and to direct the group's attention to that person. If you address questions to the group as a whole, those who like to talk will always respond first and others might not participate at all. Or several people may start talking at the same time. Put a check mark by a participant's name each time he or she speaks. Then you can call on participants who talk less often to get them involved.

Recording Initial Responses to Your Basic Question

You will begin discussion by asking the basic question you have prepared. Have participants write down the question and record their initial answers. Then, after a few minutes or when everyone seems ready, repeat the question and ask one participant, by name, to give his or her answer. Having participants write down the basic question makes them pay close attention to its specific wording; getting them to record their preliminary answers helps them collect their thoughts. But be sure to emphasize that these early answers are merely the beginning of discussion and by no means should participants feel they must remain committed to their initial ideas. On the contrary, having a record of their first thoughts lets members of the group see how opinions often undergo revision when people share their thinking.

Of course, this procedure can be modified depending upon the age of your participants and their reading and writing abilities. If your group is composed of younger children or includes students reading below grade level, rather than ask students to write down your opening question, you might want to distribute copies of it beforehand. In short, use your judgment to eliminate needless frustrations that might distract your participants from their main task—communicating their ideas about the selection in response to your basic question.

Conducting the Discussion

To lead successfully, you need to be involved with the ideas and opinions your participants express. Throughout discussion, you must assess each comment, follow up comments with questions that further discussion, and keep the group moving toward answering your basic question. The general guidelines below will help you accomplish these goals.

Guidelines for Leaders

Lead slowly.

Listen carefully to your participants' comments.

Use your seating chart regularly to note ideas.

Encourage participants to talk to one another.

Relate ideas to each other and to the basic question.

Turn to the text frequently.

Be open to challenges to any assumptions in your questions.

Give everyone a chance to contribute.

Ask follow-up questions often.

Lead slowly. Participants need time to consider the ideas that come up in discussion. If you lead too quickly, calling for new opinions before ideas have been fully clarified or explored, many of your participants will offer inadequate or irrelevant answers or will not respond at all. There are several ways you can keep discussion from moving too fast. Pause for a few seconds after asking a question; when participants answer, help them clarify their responses before you move on. If someone missed a comment, ask the participant who offered the idea to repeat it. Check frequently to see if others understand what is being said. Take the time to frame a follow-up question carefully or to rephrase one that does not seem to be clear to your participants. Let the group hear you think out loud. Taking notes and referring to the comments on your seating chart will also slow the pace of discussion.

Listen carefully to your participants' comments. Try not to be so concerned about what to ask next that you miss what is being said. Your participants' ideas—together with your own thorough preparation—are your best source of follow-up questions. When you follow up participants' comments, don't paraphrase or summarize what they have said. This tends to put words in participants' mouths and can make them feel that you will be doing their thinking for them. Pay close attention to their wording; the exact phrasing they use might suggest subtle differences of opinion or new ways to relate one comment to another. Listening intently also communicates to your participants that their thoughts are valuable.

Use your seating chart regularly to note ideas. Jotting down the comments that you want to pursue immediately, as well as those you decide to table until later, keeps good ideas from getting lost and lets you give recognition to the participants who initiated them. By keeping track of who said what, you can ask, for example, "Kathy, why do you disagree with what Sam said before, that Jack is a thief?" Or, "So, Peggy, are you agreeing with Michael that Jack climbs up again because he's bored?" When participants hear names attached to ideas and opinions, they begin to listen to each other and use each other's thinking to build interpretations. Displaying your filled-out chart when discussion is over will help make your group aware of how their comments contributed to a fuller understanding of a selection.

Encourage participants to talk to one another. In Shared Inquiry Discussion, participants broaden their individual interpretations of a text by exchanging ideas about its meaning. Encourage this exchange by getting participants to ask each other questions and to answer each other directly, rather than through you. Say, "Donna, could you tell Jason why you disagree with his point that . . . ?" Or, "Sam, would you explain to Kathy why you think differently?" In this way, you reinforce participants' responsibility for the content and success of Shared Inquiry Discussion, and you emphasize your own role as a fellow inquirer.

Relate ideas to each other and to the basic question. Give your discussion continuity and coherence by asking questions that help your participants see the relationships among ideas. Highlight possible connections between opinions your participants have expressed. Ask, "Jason, is what you just said different from what Roberto said, that . . . ?" Or, "Lisa, are you agreeing with Jason's point that . . . or Roberto's idea that . . . ?" Let your group see you thinking out loud about the relationships you notice.

Be persistent about getting your group to find satisfactory answers to your basic question. Stay with a basic question until you believe it has been fully explored. Ask questions that help your participants relate their current thinking to the basic question: "Jessica, can you explain how your idea that Jack is greedy helps us answer the opening question?" Keep everyone on track by occasionally repeating the basic question. If you leave a basic question, be willing to return to it if someone indicates that there is more to say.

Turn to the text frequently. Make a habit of getting participants to locate and read aloud passages that support what they say. Ask, "Tim, where is that line in the story about Jack's not being content?" Or, "Peggy, what in the story makes you think that Jack likes adventure?" Going back frequently to the text helps participants pick up details that they may have forgotten, or that they missed during their own reading. It also gives everyone a chance to check opinions offered in discussion against the evidence in the selection.

Be open to challenges to any assumptions in your questions. You are free to incorporate reasonable assumptions in your interpretive questions, but your participants are also free to object to them. Your assumption may involve an idea that some participants do not agree with or may not yet see for themselves. Consider this a useful opportunity: if a participant seems uncomfortable with a question, ask why. Sorting out the reasons for your disagreement will help clarify the problem to be discussed.

Give everyone a chance to contribute. Try to call on each participant several times. Marking your seating chart when someone speaks will help you keep track of participation. Do not let a few articulate students dominate discussion; make it a point to address questions to those who speak rarely or not at all. In time, shy students can become eager participants if you make a gentle but persistent effort to draw them out.

Ask follow-up questions often. Follow-up questions are your "contact" with your participants. Your consistent questioning keeps participants attentive to the central problem and helps them refine their answers. It is through your careful questioning that you and your participants come to understand the selection better.

Asking Effective Follow-up Questions

To come up with follow-up questions that lead to a greater understanding of
the selection, listen to what each participant is saying. Think each comment
through: Is the participant's idea clear? Is it relevant? Does it need to be
supported with evidence from the selection? Are others in the group likely
to understand it? Does it have implications for answering your basic question?
Asking yourself these kinds of questions will help you determine what
follow-up question to use. Consider this exchange:

> *Leader:*   Michael, why does Jack trade the cow for the beans?
>
> *Michael:*   I think that he wants to get away from his mother.
>
> *Leader:*   What in the story makes you think he wants to get
> away from his mother?

Here the leader has asked Michael to support his answer with evidence from
the selection. Another appropriate follow-up might be to request clarification:
"What do you mean when you say Jack wants to 'get away'?" Or the leader
might pursue an implication in Michael's comment: "Does Jack resent the way
his mother treats him?" The leader can choose the question that seems best
in the context of the discussion, perhaps returning to a second follow-up
question later.

Follow-up questions don't have to be perfectly worded. If your question
isn't clear, your participants will let you know, and you can then rephrase
it or try another. Take your time in thinking of questions, and concentrate on
what your participants are saying. You don't have to follow up on every idea;
experienced leaders generally ask one follow-up question for every two or three
of their participants' responses. The important thing is to develop a habit
of listening carefully and following up with questions.

There are many ways to use follow-up questions in discussion.

To clarify comments. Much of what your participants say may need clarification; they need time—and your help—to formulate their responses clearly. Many times participants do not say exactly what they mean, or they offer what appear to be superficial comments. By asking one or more follow-up questions, you help participants articulate their ideas more clearly. If you do not understand a comment, or if you notice puzzled looks, then ask the speaker to elaborate on the initial statement or to repeat it in different words: "Peggy, what do you mean when you say Jack needs adventure?" Question any special use of language, especially clichés or slang that some members of the group may not find familiar. This effort to clarify is essential to good discussion, and your participants will soon grow to feel comfortable with it. They will come to understand that you want to clarify their ideas because you are genuinely interested in exploring them.

To substantiate opinions. Not all opinions offered during your discussion will be equally valid. Some opinions will be better substantiated by evidence from the selection than others. By asking participants to recall or read relevant passages that support what they say, you encourage more attentive reading and help ensure that discussion is closely tied to the text. Thus, if a participant asserts that "Jack is greedy," you might ask, "What in the story makes you think that Jack is greedy, Donna?" Often you will want to ask how or why the evidence supports the participant's opinion. If Donna answered, "It says here, 'Jack was not content,' " you might ask, "Why does 'not content' make you think Jack is greedy?"

To solicit additional opinions. Get your participants involved by asking them whether they agree or disagree with a comment under consideration. Ask, "Toby, do you agree with Jennifer's point that . . . ?" or "Don, how would you answer the question I just asked Lisa?" Then follow up on the answers they give. Participants may offer the same opinion but have different reasons and different evidence for it. Such differences may indicate new avenues for exploration.

When you ask participants for additional opinions, your task is not merely to add them to the discussion; you want to try to build relationships among the new ideas and those already offered. After a new idea has been explained, try to ask a question to link it back to earlier comments: "Sam, is your idea that Jack climbed up the third time to get more money different from Tony's idea that Jack just wanted to take care of his mother?"

To develop an idea by pursuing its implications. Your participants may fail to see all the consequences of their own thinking. If you feel that an idea expressed in discussion has important implications, use a follow-up question to draw them out. In the following exchange, the leader is making an effort to get at the train of thought behind an interpretation:

> *Leader:* Donna, why does Jack climb the beanstalk the third time?
>
> *Donna:* He gets greedy. On the second trip, he steals the hen that lays golden eggs. He wouldn't have to climb the stalk as long as the hen lived.
>
> *Leader:* Does having the hen make him greedy?

By pursuing the implications of what your participants say, you help them enlarge and clarify their opinions. And, in the process, you uncover more ideas for your group to consider.

To test whether an idea is consistent with the facts. The most satisfying interpretations of a selection are those that account for all the relevant facts. It is a good idea, therefore, to have your participants consider evidence that might contradict their opinions or require them to modify their positions. For example:

Leader: Laura, why does Jack succeed in this story?

Laura: It's all luck. Good things just happen to Jack.

Leader: If it's all luck, why does the author refer to Jack as "sharp as a needle"?

There is no intent here to prove that the response is wrong. By inquiring into the validity of an answer, you are only helping the participant think about whether an idea is consistent with all the evidence in the text. In the above example, in response to the leader's follow-up question, Laura might say, "He's being sarcastic. Jack isn't sharp, he's dumb. The author is making fun of Jack." Here, the leader's follow-up question has uncovered more fully the participant's point of view. By testing interpretations, you help your participants develop the flexibility to expand upon or reconsider their initial assumptions and judgments.

To select a line of inquiry. At any given moment in discussion, there are usually more good ideas expressed than you can work with at one time. Two participants may state opinions, one right after another, or one participant may offer a response with two good ideas in it, both worth pursuing. Decide which idea to pursue—keeping in mind both your basic question and your group's need for coherence in discussion—and then ask an appropriate follow-up question. To make sure you don't forget ideas that you may want to pursue later, and to assure participants that their thoughts will not be lost or forgotten, jot them down on your seating chart. When you return to an idea, refer to the person who introduced it: "Michael said earlier. . . ."

Closing Discussion

By the end of Shared Inquiry Discussion, you want your group to have heard and discussed a number of answers to your basic interpretive question, and for all participants to be able to give their own answers and support them with evidence from the text. Since basic questions can have several satisfactory answers, it is likely that members of your group will end up with different opinions. Having thoroughly discussed an interpretive question does not imply reaching total agreement, or even a majority opinion, about how best to answer it.

One way of closing discussion is to repeat the basic question and call on members of the group to give answers they remember hearing. This is a time for participants to recognize what interpretations have evolved as well as what might be discussed further. Often new ideas are discovered.

Participants may want to look back at their original written answers to see if their opinions have changed. Ask if anyone had an answer that was not discussed. This is also a good time to call on members of the group who did not participate very much ("Jessica, did you hear an answer that made sense to you?"). After your participants review the answers they remember, check your chart for any additional answers and ask participants about them: "Bill, didn't you have a different answer, something about . . . ?" Or, "Kathy, what was that other point you made about . . . ?"

Encourage your participants to take a moment to formulate or even write down their final answers to the basic question, taking into account the opinions and evidence offered by other members of the group. This synthesis is occurring naturally all through discussion, but now is the time to emphasize that even the most confidently held opinions can be improved by the ideas of others. Ask if anyone arrived at an answer that differs substantially from the one that he or she wrote down at the start of discussion. Then ask those participants who changed their minds to identify the ideas that seemed especially persuasive. Your participants will value shared inquiry more when they pause to consider how their own thinking has developed over the course of discussion.

Shared inquiry is a thinking process that does not necessarily end when discussion time is up. In fact, having successful discussions should inspire further reflection; writing after discussion is one of the ways you can encourage your participants to continue their interpretive work on a selection.

Sharing Questions Discussion: A Variant for Read-Aloud Participants

For participants in the Read-Aloud program, we recommend Sharing Questions Discussion—an adaptation of Shared Inquiry Discussion. Begin Sharing Questions Discussion by writing on the board or on chart paper five or six of the questions you intend to lead. Writing your questions on the board, in the order you intend to ask them, will help children follow the discussion and focus on each question as it is being discussed. Read aloud each question in turn, and ask for answers. Through follow-up questions, explore why students came up with their answers. When several answers are given to an interpretive question, ask other children if they agree or disagree with what they have heard. Try to foster an exchange of opinion and develop a few strong answers.

As in Shared Inquiry Discussion, you will want to encourage students to give reasons for their answers by referring to the text. Children need not read a passage in order to substantiate their opinions—recalling a line or a part of the text and paraphrasing it for the group is perfectly acceptable. If children have difficulty doing this at first, by all means reread the passage you think they might have in mind, and ask whether it supports their answer. This should quickly get them in the habit of referring to the story themselves. As their listening and reading skills develop, so will their ability to find and cite evidence on their own.

After a number of responses have been given to a question, ask children whether they have each heard an answer that satisfies them. If some students indicate that they are not yet satisfied, have them contribute additional answers at this time. Then proceed to the next question. Conclude Sharing Questions Discussion by reiterating that all the opinions offered helped everyone understand the story or poem better.

3

Working with Your Participants in Shared Inquiry

Leading shared inquiry holds many rewards, but it is also a substantial challenge. This chapter offers suggestions for improving your skills as a leader so that you can deepen your participants' shared inquiry experience.

AVOIDING COMMON MISTAKES

Shared inquiry learning will be different for you as well as for your students. Even though new leaders come away from the Basic Leader Training Course with a good understanding of the principles of shared inquiry and eager to put them into practice, they can sometimes make the following mistakes.

Not focusing on interpretation. One of the most difficult things to grasp about shared inquiry is that just getting your participants talking is not enough. While it is a good first step, in shared inquiry the ideas must always be focused on the text.

Many questions that can generate conversation and even heated debate will not help you reach the goal of increasing students' higher-level reading comprehension. Remember, questions that ask students to speculate about "what happens next" (i.e., after the story is over), or about what students would do in a situation similar to one faced by the main character, tend to distract them from the story. So does moving too quickly to evaluation—to questions that ask participants to judge characters or the author before they are fully understood. By concentrating on interpretive questions, you will better help participants learn how to read and understand challenging texts.

Not probing ideas in depth. The informal atmosphere of shared inquiry should not prevent you from asking your students to think critically. One mistake new leaders often make is that of merely polling the group for answers, asking a follow-up question of each, and not knowing what to do next. Instead, you need to move the group forward by insisting that students provide reasons and evidence for their opinions. Once students understand that you will be probing their ideas in depth, they will meet your high expectations.

Asking leading questions. Shared inquiry depends on a special relationship between students and teacher. As a shared inquiry leader, you do not know the best answers to the interpretive questions you ask. It is essential that you keep an open mind about what is important in the work in order to maintain an authentic learning situation in which you ask questions to learn from—and not just to test—your students. Leading participants to a "right" way of looking at the text, making sure they get the lesson of the story or absorb your point of view on a work of nonfiction, will soon undermine your efforts to help students think for themselves.

For shared inquiry to work, your group members must feel that all their ideas and sudden insights—even their mistakes—are valuable steps in the process of building an interpretation. When participants feel confident that even their tentative opinions will be treated with respect, they will be more willing to risk speaking up.

Insufficient preparation. It cannot be overemphasized that in shared inquiry your own direct, patient, and thoughtful encounter with the text— your careful reading, note taking, and preparation of your own interpretive questions—is essential to being a successful leader. Without sufficient preparation you will not be able to ask effective follow-up questions that lead participants to read more closely and involve themselves in the problems of meaning you raise. This is true not only with regard to the writings of the philosophers in Introduction to Great Books and the Great Books program for adults, but also to the folk and fairy tales in Junior Great Books.

In shared inquiry you provide a model of a reader who is curious about a problem and interested in pursuing a solution. Over time, your participants will come to adopt the habits of mind you display—flexibility, open-mindedness, persistence, and curiosity. Demonstrating these attitudes throughout the program will have as much impact on your students as any individual discussion you might lead or particular skill you might teach.

PREPARING WITH A COLLEAGUE OR CO-LEADER

Working with a partner will make your preparation more enjoyable; it will also make you a more confident leader. If you have a co-leader, you should always meet with him or her sometime before your Shared Inquiry Discussion to review your prepared interpretive questions. If you have no co-leader, it is an excellent idea to meet with a colleague who has agreed to read the selection and talk it over with you. This "prediscussion" gives you the opportunity to share your thinking about a selection, refine your questions, generate new ones, and develop clusters. It is also the best way to try out your questions to decide which ones you will ask your group.

When you meet, bring along all your notes and the questions you have written. Test your questions on each other, checking to see whether they might be answered in more than one way based on the selection. Keep track of where you find relevant evidence in the text; later, during discussion, the page numbers you have jotted down will make it easier to direct participants to important passages. If the two of you strongly disagree about how to answer a question, it is often an excellent one to ask your group. Also, exploring differences between your interpretations will sometimes help you come up with new and more interesting questions.

As you go through your questions, continue to rethink and improve them. Then select your best questions and check them to make sure they are clear, specific, and thought-provoking. Sort the questions into clusters, following the steps suggested in the previous chapter. Finally, choose the cluster that you will use to start discussion.

Distance often improves judgment, so try to let a day or two pass between writing and reviewing your questions. You might also want to compare your questions to those published in the Teacher's Edition or Leader's Guide; these can supplement your thinking, serving as another point of view when you are ready to decide which questions you want to ask in discussion.

READING ALOUD TO YOUR STUDENTS

A good way to help students get the most out of shared inquiry is to allow time to read the selection aloud to them. We recommend this not only for the primary grades, but also for older students. This practice enables students to concentrate on the story being told rather than on the mechanics of reading, and helps them fix the plot in their minds. It also gives students confidence in their ability to understand the language and ideas of the story when they return to it for a second reading and note taking. Younger children especially enjoy repeated readings of a well-loved story; but even in high school, your reading can help motivate students and enable them to pick up challenging vocabulary in context as well as conveying to them a sense of the author's style.

While reading to your students, do not ask "prediction" questions. Such questions lead students to guess what the author will say next—and in shared inquiry, children are encouraged not to speculate, but to base their opinions on the text.

By hearing the Junior Great Books selections read aloud, students can more readily comprehend even difficult vocabulary and sentence structure. Selections in the program are not chosen according to readability formulas, but rather for their age-appropriateness and appeal, and their potential for supporting interpretive discussion. Students' experience with selections that are rich in language and style will result in a growing sophistication of expression on their part.

WORKING WITH CHALLENGING VOCABULARY

Junior Great Books selections have not been simplified to meet a controlled vocabulary; the words appear exactly as the author or translator wrote them. Brief glosses for some words are provided in the Teacher's Editions for the younger grades so that teachers can give students quick definitions during the first reading. But because the range of vocabulary in the selections is exceptionally broad, students may need further help in dealing with unfamiliar words, and with familiar words that are used in unfamiliar ways.

As you read the selection in preparation for your work on a unit, you will begin to notice vocabulary that might be new to your participants. In looking over these words, try to distinguish between those that are significant to the meaning of the story or essay and those that seem less central to it. You may find yourself doing this naturally as you think about the interpretive problems that interest you. Some words, unusual or fairly ordinary, will give you pause, while others, though perhaps more exotic, will not raise your curiosity. We can explain this distinction more clearly by looking at some words in "Cinderella" (Junior Great Books Series Two, Second Semester) that are almost certainly unfamiliar to students reading at grade level:

aglow	garret
brooch	haughtiest
cinders	liveried
coiffed	parquet
endured	unsurpassed

Some of these words help create the setting or mood of the story, but do not figure in important interpretive issues in the work. Perhaps *coiffed, liveried, parquet,* and *brooch* fit this description for you. Children will probably find, as you do, that these words are not essential to their understanding of the story, and will read right over them and figure out rough meanings from context. For example, reading that the stepsisters had "rooms with parquet floors," or that Cinderella, instead of leaving their hair "in a tangle," "coiffed them to perfection," children will gather that *parquet* is fancy flooring, and that *coiffed* is related to having nicely styled hair.

Showing students how to search the context for clues to a word's meaning and asking them questions that guide them to do so are the best ways of encouraging them to grasp this less significant vocabulary. Asking participants to memorize definitions for a long list of words chosen randomly from the selection will only deflect them from their search for meaning in the story as a whole; besides, by removing the words from context, you remove the students' impetus for learning them. These "background" words, though never defined precisely and perhaps forgotten when the book is closed, serve their purpose by conveying to young readers a sense of style.

But there is another category of unfamiliar words—those that seem directly related to problems of meaning—that will be in the "foreground" of your thinking about a selection. It is easy to see how readers of "Cinderella" might want to consider the meanings of *cinders, haughtiest,* or *unsurpassed* as they answer an interpretive question such as *Why is Cinderella kind to the stepmother and stepsisters who mistreat her?* In your preparation, you will have found the words that seem to you especially intriguing and important. In addition, your students' own ideas about the story might lead them to ask about or comment on words that had not caught your attention but that seem to deserve the group's careful thought. Sharing students' questions in class after the first reading will give participants an opportunity to bring up these words and begin to think about them.

Words that appear to you or your participants as key terms to interpret should be explored during the course of Shared Inquiry Discussion. To do this effectively, deal with a difficult word as you would any point needing clarification. First ask for a rough definition—participants' own or the dictionary's. (The rules of discussion do not permit you to offer one.) Then, in follow-up questions, inquire about the word's connotations in context, and the author's possible reasons for using that particular word rather than another. Guide participants to relate what is said about the word to the interpretive question being discussed. In this way, they will see how the meaning of a word both derives from and contributes to the context in which it is used.

Seemingly commonplace words may carry a great weight of meaning within a given work, for example, the word *beautiful* in "Cinderella." This is especially true of the Introduction to Great Books selections for high school and college students. The meaning of well-known words such as *conscience, judgment,* and *instinct* may seem elusive as used in Immanuel Kant's "Conscience" (Third Series). "The Declaration of Independence" (Second Series) abounds with long words such as *annihilation, consanguinity,* and *usurpation,* but discussion might center more fruitfully on interpreting the full significance of the seemingly simple *one people,* or *right.* As your students come to see that an interpretation can turn on the possible meanings of a single word, their interest in exploring unfamiliar vocabulary will grow. In time, handling new words will become a natural and regular part of their effort to understand what they read.

TEXTUAL ANALYSIS: HELPING YOUR GROUP EXAMINE A PASSAGE IN DETAIL

Textual analysis is a methodical way to look closely at a passage in a story or essay. In textual analysis, a group discusses a single passage line by line and sometimes word by word, raising questions about its meaning.

Textual analysis should be a regular part of Shared Inquiry Discussion. It may be done any time your question or a participant's evidence focuses the group's attention on a specific passage in the selection. When participants are having an especially hard time with a text, textual analysis can help them get a foothold. Ask them where their difficulty lies, or choose a passage yourself that seems important and challenging. Good possibilities for textual analysis are the opening or close of a selection, a crisis or a change of direction, or paragraphs that contain words and phrases the author seems to use in a special way.

To conduct textual analysis, ask someone to read the passage aloud if it is short, while other members of the group follow in their books. This focuses attention and may give some participants the beginning of an understanding of what the passage means. Then ask questions to help the group review the context. In a story, ask who is speaking in the passage—author, fictional narrator, or character—and recall what incidents have occurred up to that point. In nonfiction, ask about the position of the passage in the argument as a whole. If the passage is at the beginning, consider its purpose there. Does it introduce key terms or state the author's purpose? Does it describe a problem the author hopes to solve?

Next, go over the passage line by line, discussing any word, phrase, or sentence that puzzles or interests you or your participants. Essentially, you are brainstorming ideas about what the passage might mean. Untangle difficult sentences by asking about separate clauses or phrases. Work on difficult words by asking questions about their meaning in context and letting participants contribute their own or dictionary definitions. Invite your group to consider the author's specific choice of words; ask, "Why did the author select this particular way to say it?" Examine metaphors by asking about the comparisons they set up and their implications. While doing all this, try to remain open to all possibilities of meaning. Because every word in the story represents a decision the author has made, assume for the moment that everything might have importance in your understanding of the whole.

Becoming an Interpretive Reader

Encourage participants to contribute questions and to answer each other's questions if they can. Not all of their questions will be useful. Some may have factual answers that the group will readily supply. And others will have no answer at all in the text. In the process of asking questions, though, your group may uncover one or two new interpretive problems that can contribute significantly to discussion. Allow the group to discuss these briefly, and if they seem interesting, write them down so you can go back to them after you have worked through the whole passage.

When the passage has been examined, ask participants if they can relate any new discoveries to what has already been discussed. Bring up again one of your prepared interpretive questions or return to one of the more interesting questions that your group raised during textual analysis.

Below are a leader's notes on a passage from Richard Wilbur's "A Game of Catch," indicating the kinds of questions that could be raised in textual analysis.

Why does Scho sit in the tree?

Why does he grin? What's he feeling?

"One minute to go," said Monk, with a fraction of a grin. Scho stood up and watched the ball slap back and forth for several minutes more, and then he turned and pulled himself up into the crotch of the tree.

"Where are you going?" Monk asked.

Why does Monk ask? (Does he feel guilty??)

"Just up the tree," Scho said.

"I guess he doesn't want to catch," said Monk.

Why does Monk say this? Why doesn't Scho reply? Why isn't Glennie saying anything?

Scho went up and up through the fat light-gray branches until they grew slender and bright and gave under him. He found a place where several supple branches were knit to make a (dangerous) chair, and sat there with his head coming out of the leaves into the sunlight. He could see the two other boys down below, the ball going back and forth between them as if they were bowling on the grass, and Glennie's crew-cut head looking like a sea urchin.

Why does Scho choose a dangerous seat? To prove himself? To make the boys worry?

What is Scho feeling looking down at the boys? Why does he keep on watching the boys' game?

MAINTAINING YOUR ROLE AS LEADER

The spontaneity and independent thinking that make shared inquiry so exciting can also create some challenges for the leader. But maintaining your role as leader is what establishes the atmosphere for your group to share ideas and think through interpretive problems. When difficulties arise, as they do for even the most experienced leaders, continue to work within the framework of the rules of Shared Inquiry Discussion. Asking follow-up questions, just as you ordinarily do, should help you solve most types of problems.

Because participants are encouraged to think freely, a common problem leaders face is when participants' comments stray from the text and a search for its meaning. When participants answer a question about a story by talking about themselves and their own experiences, ask a follow-up question to get them thinking again about the text:

> *Leader:* Kyle, why does Scho choose a "dangerous seat" when he climbs into the tree?
>
> *Kyle:* It's dangerous to climb too high up in a tree. When I climb high up in a tree, I get scared.
>
> *Leader:* Well, do you think Scho knows he is in danger high up in the tree?
>
> *Kyle:* I don't think so, because it says he jounced up and down. He wouldn't do that if he was afraid.

Keep in mind that what seems like a digression may actually reflect a leap of mind into new territory. If you're not sure of the relevance of a response, ask the participant to furnish the connection. Asking participants to explain how their responses relate to the original question will prevent you from overlooking worthwhile ideas.

Sometimes a student will respond to one of your questions by saying, "I don't know." This lack of response may simply mean that the participant didn't understand the question. Try rephrasing it:

Leader:	Why does Scho enlarge the scope of his game at the end of the story?
Shawn:	I don't know.
Leader:	At the end of the story, why does Scho say, "I want you to do whatever you're going to do for the whole rest of your life"?

Sometimes, when you rephrase your question, it may be helpful to give a participant a choice of alternatives that reflect your doubt:

Leader:	Why does Scho climb the tree when Glennie and Monk don't let him play?
Jordan:	I don't know.
Leader:	Do you think Scho was angry when he climbed the tree, or maybe embarrassed?
Jordan:	I think he might have felt embarrassed because he got left out. And so he climbed the tree to get their attention and show off.

Often, all the participant needs is additional time to let the question sink in. After a pause, if you continue to get no response, think of a passage that might clarify the problem and ask the participant to read it aloud. Then repeat your question. Try to stay with that person as long as you feel you are accomplishing something in striving for an answer. Then ask other participants to help out.

If participants forget important details or offer interpretations based on a misreading of the text, use follow-up questions to help them recall the facts. Ask your participants to read and examine closely a relevant passage. This is also a good strategy when participants cannot locate the facts they need to support a reasonable opinion. Make sure your participants keep their books open throughout discussion. Encourage them to refer to the text often to look for examples and to check ideas.

If participants are having difficulty understanding a particular word or phrase in a selection—and this becomes important in discussion—then use the word in a follow-up question meant to get students thinking about it. For instance, if students are not sure what the word *meek* means when applied to a character, ask them to describe that character and how he or she acts in different situations. Then ask, "Melissa, is that what *meek* means? Do you think a meek person acts in the way you've described?" This will give students a fuller concept of the word, and by asking them to present a clearer picture of the character, you will be leading them more deeply into the story. If your group requires a more formal definition, ask someone to look the word up, but continue discussion until the dictionary definition can be introduced. Then ask participants to relate the dictionary meaning of the word to how it's used in the story. "Jeremy, can you think of times when Cinderella acts 'patient' and 'humble'?"

With experience, you will learn other ways to solve problems through follow-up questions. For instance, participants who dominate discussion can create problems by intimidating shy or less articulate participants into complete silence. You can check this in a positive, productive way by asking someone else to evaluate or comment upon one of the ideas offered by the too voluble participant ("Alex, can you wait just a minute? Maria, do you agree with what Alex just said, that . . . ?"). This strategy gets everyone's attention. It also selects a portion of the response to pursue, slows the rush of ideas, and involves other participants. You can also ask talkative participants to respond to ideas they have not originated, thus encouraging them to listen more patiently to others in the group.

Participants who are initially shy and hesitant about expressing their ideas, or who tend merely to agree with their friends, can be drawn out if you show that their insights are useful to the group. Return to the ideas that they do express, and ask others in the group to consider them: "Ann, do you agree with Jennifer's idea that . . . ?" Be persistent in directing questions to them by name and listening carefully to what they say.

There are also simple strategies for handling other kinds of problems that arise in discussion. In some cases, there may be a general lack of interest in your basic question or all of your participants may seem stumped by it. Take some time to let the question take hold before deciding to drop it. Try rephrasing the question, or ask your participants to read aloud a passage that originally suggested the question to you. This may help them to see what the problem of meaning is. You might also want to check your cluster for another question that would help your participants begin to answer your basic question. If the group seems to be having trouble with the subject matter of the basic question, ask questions to find out exactly what the difficulty is.

If your participants are resisting the selection as a whole, follow up specifically on why they didn't like it or couldn't get into it. Did they find it difficult to understand, perhaps because of unusual vocabulary or style? Did they find it boring? Did they dislike the way the characters act, or did certain incidents make them uncomfortable? Get your participants to point to passages that support their feelings, and ask them why the author included that information. What effect does it have on the rest of the story? Build on their dislike to get them into the selection. You might also want to use textual analysis of an especially difficult or important passage to help your group approach the selection. In handling this type of problem, keep in mind that liking a selection is not a prerequisite to having a good discussion. Interest in a work has a tendency to grow through shared inquiry; by working together, participants can often understand selections that put them off individually. In any event, make sure you continue to focus on an interpretive discussion of the selection. Students soon discover that they have more ideas to talk about than they initially realized.

Any Shared Inquiry Discussion—with young people or adults—will have its share of wrong turns. Handle these as part of the normal process of shared inquiry, and your participants will learn to expect such difficulties from time to time and to feel confident that there are always ways to overcome them and get back into discussion. By dealing with problems within the context of your role as leader—as an asker of questions—you'll encourage the best creative and cooperative efforts of your group. Moreover, you'll minimize inhibitions caused by the fear of failure and help make discussion a freer, more comfortable exchange of ideas.

WORKING WITH LESS-ABLE READERS

There is no better way to involve less-able readers in the higher-level thinking that occurs in Junior Great Books than to implement the full Junior Great Books Curriculum (see Chapter 4). The Curriculum was designed for use in a heterogeneous class that includes less-able readers. Its focus on interpretation makes it possible for each student to work starting from his or her own level of ability. The Curriculum's range of interpretive activities allows students of different learning styles to work from their strengths, while gaining practice in areas of weaker skills. However, if your program consists only of Shared Inquiry Discussion, the following suggestions, which draw on the Curriculum activities, will help you involve less-able readers.

> *Give students a chance to hear the story read aloud several times.* When they grasp the story as a whole, students will work more confidently on both decoding and comprehension. You might read the story aloud in class two or even three times, or make a tape recording which students can use on their own in a "listening corner." If students participate in pull-out enrichment classes, ask their teachers to use Curriculum activities for some of their work.

Students can also help each other read, by working in pairs or small groups and prompting each other when needed. In some schools, older students serve as reading tutors to help beginners.

Make time for students to ask questions. Setting aside a few minutes after the first reading of a story for students to ask questions and share their reactions provides you with the opportunity to resolve some of their difficulties. Give students time to put their questions into words. If they look puzzled, ask them if they would like to hear part of the story again. Writing their questions helps less-able students clear up specific problems and set an agenda for active reading. Check over written questions immediately so that you can address factual questions early on. Another possibility is to arrange students' questions in groups on a Junior Great Books bulletin board, so students get a sense of the issues their classmates see in the story.

Add dramatizations or interpretive art activities to your students' preparation. Choose dramatic moments for students to act out or illustrate, and lead short discussions that bring out students' different interpretations. You might want to couple these activities with a brief textual analysis.

Keep the focus on interpretation. Interpretive questions are actually easier to start answering than factual ones because each student can draw on whatever part of the story he or she recalls best, rather than having to remember the specific detail a factual question intends to elicit. Answering interpretive questions helps readers see details in a story as important and interesting, because they contribute to the meaning of the whole.

Maintain high expectations for Shared Inquiry Discussion and don't assume that your students are "not ready" for such a high-level activity. Lead a small group, giving each student many chances to speak. Show sincere interest in participants' ideas by encouraging them to explain and give reasons for their answers. Help out by directing them to passages that might provide evidence.

Involve students' parents. Be sure the parents of your less-able students understand how much their children have to gain from Junior Great Books, and that reading with their children can assure full involvement in the program. Students will work more confidently and progress more rapidly on both decoding and comprehension the more they are read to at home.

ASSESSING YOUR STUDENTS' PROGRESS

Participants in Junior Great Books will have a clearer idea of what is expected of them if from time to time you guide them in assessing how well they listened and responded to each other in their Shared Inquiry Discussions. Did they strive to pinpoint and resolve the story's important interpretive problems? Did they consider answers opposed to their own, and weigh the evidence in support of each possibility? Ask students for examples of how their notes helped them remember an idea or find evidence to support an opinion. You can use the notes on your seating chart to help them answer these questions.

After Shared Inquiry Discussion, call attention to the times when a participant who offered an opinion only tentatively triggered an important insight in someone else. Illustrate how ideas are continually reevaluated by helping your group recall opinions that were abandoned and later, as a result of new insights, were found to have value. Remind participants that in discussion many ideas must be pooled before a satisfying interpretation can be realized, and that it is necessary to be open to change if the evidence demands it.

A good sign that participants are starting to feel comfortable with Shared Inquiry Discussion is that they no longer respond exclusively to you; they talk directly to each other. They help each other out, suggesting relevant evidence or lines of reasoning to support answers. Perhaps they will even anticipate some of your follow-up questions by asking fellow participants for clarification or evidence. When participants see they can contribute to Shared Inquiry Discussion by working with each other's ideas as well as their own, they will become more attentive listeners and more active readers and thinkers.

TRANSCRIPT OF A SAMPLE DISCUSSION

The following transcript from parts of a Shared Inquiry Discussion of "Jack and the Beanstalk" includes marginal notes to show how follow-up questions were used to deepen participants' thinking. As you read through the transcript, think about how you would respond to what the participants say. In each instance, several different follow-up questions are possible.

The cluster below will help you see what ideas the leader grappled with when preparing questions for discussion. You will notice that at appropriate points in the discussion the leader makes use of a few of these cluster questions to follow up on participants' ideas. A prepared cluster can be an important resource if it is used properly. But don't rely so heavily on your cluster questions that you ignore the responses of your participants. Prepared questions can never take the place of your on-the-spot follow-up questions, which reflect your reactions to what is being said. However, if you have prepared well, you will be able to trust your ability to recall the interpretive issues in the story, and you will probably use some of your cluster questions spontaneously, when they seem to fit naturally in the context of the discussion.

> *Basic Question: Why does Jack climb the beanstalk a third time?*
>
> 1. *Why isn't Jack "content" even though he has a limitless supply of gold from the magic hen?*
>
> 2. *Does Jack return a third time because he enjoys outsmarting the ogre?*
>
> 3. *Why isn't Jack afraid of being eaten by the ogre?*
>
> 4. *Why does Jack risk his life by taking the singing harp?*

Soon after asking the basic question, the leader discovers that the group almost unanimously views Jack's primary motivation as greed and his risk-taking as selfish. Since the leader would not have asked the basic question if she had thought that it had only one reasonable answer, her challenge was to help make participants aware, through careful questioning, that the matter under discussion is more complex than participants' immediate answers suggest.

Leader: [*after asking the basic question and having the group write down answers*] Alex, why does Jack determine "to have another try at his luck" by climbing the beanstalk the third time?

Alex: He got greedy.

Leader: What do you mean by "got greedy"?

Asks for clarification.

Alex: Well, he wasn't greedy the first two times. But by the third time he had the hen that would lay golden eggs. He wouldn't have to climb the stalk as long as the hen lived.

Leader: If he wasn't greedy at first, why do you think he became greedy?

Pursues an implication of Alex's response.

• • •

As discussion continues, the leader finds that participants are unanimous so far in their response to the basic question, agreeing with Alex that Jack climbed the beanstalk a third time simply because he was greedy.

Leader: Maria, do you also agree that Jack didn't become greedy until his third trip up the beanstalk?

Solicits an additional opinion. When the leader probes Maria's response, a different definition of greed emerges.

Maria: No. He was always greedy, like earlier when the cow went dry and he didn't want to have his mother worry about money anymore.

Leader: Do you think Jack is being greedy when he wants to take care of his mother?

The leader pursues how Maria is defining greed.

Maria: Well, maybe it's not so much greedy as being afraid.

Leader: Afraid of what?

Asks for clarification.

Maria: Afraid of what the future might hold?

Leader: Then, Maria, does Jack climb the beanstalk for the third time because he is afraid of the future?

         Returns to basic question, incorporating Maria's new insight; pursues an implication of her train of thought.

Maria: Maybe. Maybe he thought the hen would stop laying just like the cow went dry.

Liz: I still think he was greedy from the very beginning. He sure wasn't thinking about anyone but himself when he made that stupid, selfish trade for the beans.

Leader: Liz, why do you think Jack was stupid to trade the dry cow for the magic beans?

         Asks for substantiation.

Liz: Well, Jack didn't know for sure that the beans were magic. He just made the trade without thinking about what his mother would say or what would happen next. Besides it's stupid to trust strange old men. In fact, I think the funny-looking man was working for the ogre. He had these beans that would make a stalk grow up to the ogre's house so he obviously went around giving them out so that the ogre would have plenty of little boys to eat.

Leader: Liz, can you show us evidence for your opinion that the old man works for the ogre?

         In order to prevent a possible digression (the old man is an agent of the ogre), the leader asks Liz to substantiate her opinion with evidence from the story.

Liz: Well, I guess I don't see any proof that the old man worked for the ogre, but I still don't think he's on Jack's side. On page 143, he says Jack is "sharp" but Jack really isn't at all. That proves the old man isn't honest.

Sam: I disagree. The old man means it when he says Jack is sharp. After all, Jack just gave a smart answer to that weird question "How many beans make five?" And besides, the old man told the truth: the beans really were magic and they helped Jack become rich.

Leader: So, Sam, was Jack being stupid and impulsive in trusting the old man or was he taking a pretty good risk?

The leader formulates a question combining Liz's and Sam's opposing points of view. In so doing, the leader makes it easier for the group to pursue the implications of Jack's risk taking, ideas that are relevant to the basic question.

. . .

Leader: Let's return now to our opening question and see what some other people have to say. Sarah, why do you think Jack went up the third time?

Asks the group to reconsider the basic question in light of the new thinking about Jack's character; solicits additional opinions.

Sarah: I think it was mostly out of greed. He realized it was easy to just go up and help himself to the giant's riches. But he also had a little bit of a sense of adventure. He wanted to outsmart the giant again . . . but the more I think about it, even that was selfish.

Steve: I think Jack is selfish, too, and always was. In the beginning of the story he doesn't have a job probably because he only thought about himself and was lazy.

Leader: Steve, if Jack was lazy, how do you account for the fact that we are told on the first page of the story that both Jack and his mother carried milk to the market every day?

Tests Steve's opinion that Jack was lazy by asking whether it is consistent with other evidence in the text. In challenging Steve's point, the leader opens the door to other interpretations of Jack.

Steve: I'll have to think about that.

Jeremy: Carrying milk every day seems like work to me. And just because Jack couldn't get a job doesn't mean he was lazy. He was probably too young. Besides, he's the one who volunteers to get work; his mother doesn't tell him to, she just wrings her hands and complains a lot.

Paula: He can't be lazy, Steve, because every time he goes up the beanstalk it says that he climbed and he climbed and he climbed and he climbed. A lazy person wouldn't have tried so hard.

Leader: That brings us back to what Sarah was saying earlier. Sarah, when you said it was "easy" for Jack to go up the third time, did you mean it wasn't dangerous . . . that Jack didn't need to be courageous and cunning?

Returns to Sarah's earlier comment to examine it in light of Paula's answer that Jack was not lazy. In asking Sarah to reconsider her thoughts about Jack, the leader pursues the line of inquiry opened up by Paula and Jeremy.

Sarah: No . . . I think he had to be smart to get away the third time. . . . In fact, I think he got smarter each time he went to the giant's.

Leader: What in the story makes you think Jack gets smarter?

Asks for substantiation.

Sarah: It says, starting on page 154, that "this time he knew better than to go straight to the ogre's house. And when he got near it he waited behind a bush till he saw the ogre's wife come out with a pail to get some water, and then he crept into the house and got into the copper."

Leader: How does that passage show that Jack is getting smarter?

Asks how the cited evidence supports Sarah's opinion.

Sarah: It shows he's planning. "He knew better than to go straight to the ogre's house." He figures the wife wouldn't be nice to him this time. And so he waits and hides until she comes out. Then he chooses a different hiding place, the copper instead of the oven.

Vanessa:	I think he's getting smarter, too. And it seems like he's enjoying himself—fooling the giant and his wife, taking the harp right from under their noses—it's like a game for him.	
Leader:	Vanessa, how can something as scary as tricking a boy-eating ogre become a kind of game for Jack?	The leader chooses a line of inquiry, asking Vanessa to clarify her "game" interpretation, rather than to elaborate on her opinion that Jack is getting smarter. This leads to a consideration of Jack's sense of adventure.
Vanessa:	Well, he has all the money he could possibly want from the hen and so, what's left for him to do except hang around the house with his mother? He can't do that forever. He needs to *do* something, take a few risks, or else he'll get bored. It was exciting the first two times up the beanstalk and so he went back to have an adventure.	
Leader:	Are you saying, Vanessa, that Jack takes this risky third trip because he is looking for kicks or because having adventures is a necessary part of growing up?	Pursues the implications in Vanessa's comments and moves the group toward the basic question.

. . .

Leader:	Emily, why does the author have Jack take a singing harp on his third trip up the beanstalk?	Having explored the complexities of Jack's character, the group was ready to examine the meaning of Jack's third trip in the context of the story as a whole.
Emily:	I don't know.	
Leader:	Well, why does Jack risk his life by taking the singing harp?	Poses a prepared cluster question, and in so doing simplifies the question to ask Emily to think about Jack's motivation rather than to consider the problem from the perspective of the author.
Emily:	I thought he took it because it was fun to take things that the giant really liked . . . and it seemed that the harp was extra special to the giant.	
Leader:	What makes you think the harp was extra special to the giant?	Asks for substantition.
Emily:	Because it made beautiful music . . . it even sang him to sleep. When Jack took the harp, it called out to the giant, "Master! Master!"	

Leader: Emily, does taking a harp that makes beautiful music show that Jack is no longer satisfied with material comforts alone?

Incorporating one of Emily's ideas, the leader returns to the problem of why Jack took the harp.

Emily: I'm not sure. . . .

Alex: Naah . . . Jack always took whatever the giant had out at the time. He would have taken anything.

Leader: But why does the author have Jack take on his third trip a singing harp—rather than some other kind of valuable object?

Reformulates the question to raise a possible intention of the author.

Emily: To show that Jack didn't just want money . . . he wanted something that was beautiful *and* magical . . . having money wasn't enough to make Jack happy.

Alex: But it says at the end of the story that Jack showed the harp to get more money.

Emily: [*to Alex*] But at least he's sharing it, not like the giant who kept it to himself. He's showing everyone that he conquered the giant and has his magic. And that's why Jack deserves to marry a princess.

Because of the leader's close interest and steady involvement, the participants in this discussion get caught up in striving for answers. They examine the text, begin to talk to one another, build on their own ideas, and come to more comprehensive interpretations of the story.

4

The Junior Great Books Curriculum
A Full Program of Interpretive Reading, Writing, and Discussion for Grades K-12

Interpretive reading is a complex habit of mind, one that needs cultivation over a period of years. For this reason, the Foundation has developed the Junior Great Books Curriculum for kindergarten through high school. The new Curriculum combines Shared Inquiry Discussion with a full complement of interpretive reading and writing activities. Together they provide a format for helping students become more accomplished readers—developing their ability to trace ideas throughout a story, to pause and reflect while they read, to look closely at meaningful words and passages, to build interpretations, and to elaborate on their ideas through writing.

The Curriculum is based on the idea that all children put forth their best intellectual efforts when they are presented with genuine problems of meaning. The interpretive activities for each Junior Great Books selection combine reading, writing, speaking, and listening, so that students reading at, above, and below grade level can develop higher-level reading and thinking skills in a whole-class setting. The activities enable students with diverse cultural and personal perspectives, learning styles, and levels of ability to contribute and learn from each other; they allow students to build steadily on their own ideas and ensure that each member of the class feels challenged and encouraged to reach his or her highest level of achievement. The strong oral component in the Curriculum—the frequent opportunities for reading aloud, and sharing notes, questions, and opinions—invites less-able readers to participate on an equal footing with the more advanced readers.

As you lead the activities in the Junior Great Books Curriculum, you will continue to focus on interpretive problems and—through your questions—encourage students to listen to and learn from each other, using the shared inquiry method taught in the Basic Leader Training Course. If you would like further instruction in conducting the Curriculum activities or improving your skills as a leader, the Foundation offers leaders one- and two-day in-depth training, which is strongly recommended for all trained leaders. The Foundation also arranges week-long institutes with individual schools or districts that are interested in curriculum reform and wish to establish a special partnership with the Foundation.

THE INTERPRETIVE ACTIVITIES

This chapter presents you with an overview of the Curriculum and its sequence of activities; complete instructions for conducting the interpretive activities can be found in the Teacher's Edition or Leader's Guide for each series. Appendix B contains sample units for various grade levels.

Prereading Questions and Text Openers

At every grade level, Curriculum teachers are provided with a brief introduction to help orient students to the selection they are about to read. In the Curriculum for grades three through twelve, students' thoughtful encounter with a work of literature begins with an activity called a Text Opener (3-6), or by answering a prereading question (7-12). These activities prime students' interest and, in some cases, prepare them to meet a potential obstacle to understanding in the selection, such as an abstract theme or metaphorical language. In all cases, Text Openers and prereading questions alert students to important interpretive issues in the text and help them connect their own experiences with the story or essay they are about to read. For instance, prior to reading "A Game of Catch," students play a game that has some parallels to Scho's, and then discuss how it feels to participate in it. For "The Melian Dialogue," students consider their own thoughts about questions such as *Which is more important—freedom or survival?* and *Do you respect people who try not to take sides in a dispute?* If students have answered the prereading question in writing, they are invited to return to it after Shared Inquiry Discussion to elaborate on or change their initial opinions, in light of their classmates' ideas—and their new understanding of the author's.

Active Reading and Taking Notes

Like you, students must read a selection twice and take notes before they are ready to interpret it. For the elementary grades and for less-able readers, at least one of the readings is done orally by the teacher while students follow along in their books. This practice enables students to concentrate on the story rather than on the mechanics of reading, and gives them confidence in their ability to understand the language and ideas of the story when they return to it for a second reading and note taking.

The activity of note taking in conjunction with a second reading is practiced throughout the Curriculum in different forms, appropriate to grade level. In the Read-Aloud program, children hear the story read the second time at home, where they discuss "G.B.'s Questions"—open-ended questions printed in the margin of their books and signalled by the Read-Aloud mascot, G.B. (pictured here). These at-home questions encourage children to pause and respond to significant moments in the story and prepare them to share their beginning ideas in class. The Curriculum for second grade continues this routine. (See the unit for "Jack and the Beanstalk," with its three at-home questions printed in the margin, in Appendix B.)

In grades three through twelve, students participate in a Directed Notes activity that asks them, during their second reading, to respond to a consistent pattern in the story or essay that helps tie the whole work together. For example, during their second reading of "A Game of Catch," students mark places where they do or do not sympathize with a character. After sharing their notes, and hearing the many different ways to interpret the actions of the three boys, students will be more prepared to address basic interpretive issues concerning Scho's motivation for playing his game, and how Glennie and Monk are involved in the conflict. For "The Melian Dialogue," students keep track of where, in their judgment, the Melians or the Athenians present a good argument. This focus guides students through a difficult text and encourages them to read more carefully and with greater sensitivity to the significance of details. By participating in Directed Notes throughout the elementary and secondary years of schooling, students internalize many different note-taking strategies, and learn how to take thoughtful notes on their own.

Sharing Questions

At every level of the Curriculum, participants are encouraged to raise their own questions about a work. Sharing Questions takes place after the first reading, to encourage students to notice and value their own reactions to a story. Sharing Questions is a time for students to clear up misreadings, get help with vocabulary, and set the selection more firmly in their minds. More important, forming questions based on their own responses gives students a starting point for interpretive thinking when they return to the selection.

Junior Great Books Teacher's Editions and Leader's Guides present a number of different options for conducting this activity. Depending on the age group, class schedule, and your own preferences, Sharing Questions is either an oral or a written activity, conducted as a whole class, in small groups, individually, or after an at-home reading with a parent.

Interpreting Words

Junior Great Books presents students with a unique opportunity to broaden their spoken and reading vocabularies. In Interpreting Words activities, presented in some form from kindergarten through grade twelve, students concentrate on the interpretive dimensions of important words. Through

Interpreting Words, students learn how specific words can contribute to understanding the broader interpretive issues of a story, and how an author's word choice can provide nuance and depth to characterization. For instance, the Interpreting Words activity for "A Game of Catch" focuses upon Scho's mixed feelings—why his game makes him feel both "exuberant and panicky." The interpretive reading sequence practiced by students in Introduction to Great Books provides them with the means to select and analyze the rich and challenging vocabulary contained in the selections.

Art and Dramatization

In the Read-Aloud program and the Curriculum for grade two, interpretive drawing and dramatizations play an important role in fostering students' imaginative and interpretive thinking about a story. In the unit for "Jack and the Beanstalk," for example, students draw their vision of the ogre. In illustrating this character, they will be expressing an interpretation of him: *Is the ogre primarily wicked and frightening? Or is he dull-witted and buffoon-like?* Which scene children choose to depict expresses their thoughts as well: a picture of the ogre listening to his golden harp conveys quite a different sense of the character than does a picture of him chasing Jack down the beanstalk.

Dramatizing scenes in a story also helps students express their ideas. In acting out a scene, they connect with unfamiliar situations, empathize with characters, and form ideas about how different characters interact with one another. For instance, students dramatizing the scene in which Jack trades the family cow for the old man's magic beans and then shows the beans to his mother, will be presenting their interpretations of all three characters: *Does the old man behave in a friendly or a mysterious manner? Does Jack agree to the trade because he is clever or just very trusting? Why isn't Jack worried about disobeying his mother?* All dramatizations and art activities conclude with students sharing and comparing their ideas. In this way they can hear perspectives different from their own, and so move forward in their thinking about the stories.

Writing After Discussion

After participating in Shared Inquiry Discussion, students are in an excellent position to assess and assimilate—through their writing—the ideas put forth during the week. From kindergarten through high school, the Curriculum provides students with support and structure for their writing. Children in the Read-Aloud program contribute to group compositions; in Junior Great Books for Series 2-6, students are given activity pages with "guiding questions" to aid them in structuring elaborated stories and essays; the interpretive reading and discussion routine itself enables students using Series 7-12 to experience an important part of the writing process—the articulation and revision of ideas—and use writing as a means of resolving interpretive and evaluative questions based on the selection. In all grades, the Curriculum prepares students to measure the opinions voiced throughout the week against their own experience and viewpoint. For example, at the conclusion of the unit for "A Game of Catch," students can assess the interpretations of Scho's conduct in the story and form a reasoned answer to the evaluative question *Is there any way to be friends with a boy like Scho?* After working on "The Melian Dialogue," students will be prepared to incorporate evidence from the text in addressing such questions as *Is it better to be idealistic or pragmatic?* and *What might countries facing Nazi Germany before World War II have learned from "The Melian Dialogue"?*

THE JUNIOR GREAT BOOKS CONTINUUM OF LEARNING

The Junior Great Books Curriculum spans all the years of schooling—enabling school systems to coordinate their reading, language arts, and critical-thinking curricula. The Junior Great Books Curriculum is comprised of three programs: the Read-Aloud program (for kindergarten and first grade), Junior Great Books (for grades two through nine), and Introduction to Great Books (for grades ten through twelve).

The Read-Aloud Program (K-1)

The Junior Great Books Read-Aloud Program is designed to help children in kindergarten and first grade experience the pleasures of reading and thinking about meaningful works of literature. The program fulfills basic reading-readiness objectives, and aids students in developing critical and imaginative thinking, comprehension, and speaking and listening skills.

In the Read-Aloud program, children focus on one unit (a story or group of poems) over a period of four to five days. Children listen as their teacher, and later a parent or adult partner, reads the story or poems to them. Because children hear the selection read aloud at least three times, all students—both nonreaders and independent readers—can participate.

Children develop and express their interpretive thinking about the selection by participating in a variety of activities, including art projects, dramatizations, and creative writing. Included in Read-Aloud units is Sharing Questions Discussion, a version of Shared Inquiry Discussion adapted for young participants.

The children's Read-Aloud books are designed so that all art and writing activities are done in them, allowing students to look over, revise, and expand upon earlier thoughts. Children learn from experience how actively responding to a story or poem and returning to both the text and their own earlier ideas enriches their insight. And books that become the child's unique intellectual product form a tangible source of pride and satisfaction for the beginning reader.

The Read-Aloud Sequence

SESSION 1

· First reading of the selection

· Sharing of initial questions and responses

· Interpretive art activity

AT-HOME WORK

· Second reading of the selection, by a parent or other adult partner, with discussion of G.B.'s Questions

· Children dictate their own "My Question" about the selection

SESSION 2

· Posting students' "My Questions"

· Third reading of the selection, with discussion of children's answers to G.B.'s Questions

· Creative activity (dramatization or art), building on the interpretive issues raised by G.B.'s Questions

SESSIONS 3 AND 4

· Sharing Questions Discussion

· Textual analysis and dramatization

· Drawing answers to interpretive questions

· Interpreting Words and art activity

· Evaluative discussion

· Group or individual writing of poems, songs, or paragraphs

The Junior Great Books Read-Aloud Program is suitable for children with widely varying abilities, and is recommended for all students. The Read-Aloud program can be used in libraries and day-care centers, as well as in school classrooms. Teachers may want to supplement the program with phonics and some basic reading comprehension instruction to have a complete literature and language arts program.

DRAGON SERIES

Volume 1

THE FROG PRINCE
Brothers Grimm as told by Wanda Gág

GUINEA FOWL AND RABBIT GET JUSTICE
*African folktale as told by Harold Courlander
and George Herzog*

"NATURE SPEAKS"
*Poetry by Carl Sandburg, James Reeves,
and Federico García Lorca*

Volume 2

FERAJ AND THE MAGIC LUTE
Arabian folktale as told by Jean Russell Larson

THE TALE OF JOHNNY TOWN-MOUSE
Beatrix Potter

"COMPANIONS"
*Poetry by A. A. Milne, Gwendolyn Brooks,
and Robert Louis Stevenson*

Volume 3

BUYA MARRIES THE TORTOISE
African folktale as told by W. F. P. Burton

THE HUCKABUCK FAMILY AND HOW THEY
RAISED POP CORN IN NEBRASKA AND
QUIT AND CAME BACK
Carl Sandburg

"MAGICAL PLACES"
*Poetry by Byrd Baylor, William Shakespeare,
and Martin Brennan*

SAILING SHIP SERIES

Volume 1

THE SHOEMAKER AND THE ELVES
Brothers Grimm as told by Wanda Gág

THE FROG WENT A-TRAVELING
Russian folktale as told by Vsevolod Garshin

"NIGHT INTO DAWN"
*Poetry by Robert Hillyer and John Ciardi,
and a Mescalero Apache song*

Volume 2

THE TALE OF TWO BAD MICE
Beatrix Potter

BOUKI CUTS WOOD
Haitian folktale as told by Harold Courlander

"FANTASY"
Poetry by Sylvia Plath, Edward Lear, and Lewis Carroll

Volume 3

LION AT SCHOOL
Philippa Pearce

COYOTE RIDES THE SUN
Native American folktale as told by Jane Louise Curry

"SEASONS"
*Poetry by Nikki Giovanni, Robert Louis Stevenson,
and Langston Hughes*

The Junior Great Books Curriculum

SUN SERIES

Volume 1

THE BLACK HEN'S EGG
French folktale as told by Natalie Savage Carlson

THE MOUSE AND THE WIZARD
Hindu fable as told by Lucia Turnbull

"IMAGINATION"
Poetry by Leslie Norris, Mark Van Doren,
and Robert Louis Stevenson

Volume 2

RUMPELSTILTSKIN
Brothers Grimm, translated by Ralph Manheim

EEYORE HAS A BIRTHDAY AND
GETS TWO PRESENTS
A. A. Milne

"WHEN I GROW UP"
Poetry by Rabindranath Tagore
and X. J. Kennedy, and a Chippewa song

Volume 3

THE KING OF THE FROGS
African folktale as told by Humphrey Harman

SNOW-WHITE AND THE SEVEN DWARFS
Brothers Grimm, translated by Randall Jarrell

"MYSTERIOUS ANIMALS"
Poetry by T. S. Eliot, Jenifer Kelly, and Robert Graves

PEGASUS SERIES

Volume 1

CHESTNUT PUDDING
Iroquois folktale as told by John Bierhorst

THE PIED PIPER
English folktale as told by Joseph Jacobs

"FANCIFUL ANIMALS"
Poetry by Edward Lear and A. A. Milne

Volume 2

THE MERMAID WHO LOST HER COMB
Scottish folktale as told by Winifred Finlay

HANSEL AND GRETEL
Brothers Grimm, translated by Randall Jarrell

"SPECIAL PLACES"
Poetry by Gwendolyn Brooks and Robert Frost,
and a Navajo poem

Volume 3

MOTHER OF THE WATERS
Haitian folktale as told by Diane Wolkstein

ZLATEH THE GOAT
Isaac Bashevis Singer

"SECRET MESSAGES"
Poetry by Robert Louis Stevenson, Barbara Juster Esbensen,
and Emily Dickinson

Read-Aloud materials:

Four nongraded series (Dragon, Sailing Ship, Sun, and Pegasus). Student books for each series contain six
stories and three groups of poems, and all activities. Teacher's Editions for each series include full instructions
for conducting the Curriculum, an annotated student text, and suggested interpretive questions for
Sharing Questions Discussion. Since children complete all writing and drawing activities in their books,
student books for all Read-Aloud series are intended to be used as consumables. Teacher's Editions
are required for implementing the Read-Aloud program.

Junior Great Books (Grades 2-9)

The Junior Great Books Curriculum for grades two through nine develops students' reading, speaking, critical-thinking, and writing skills by means of intensive work with outstanding literature from cultures around the world. By supplementing the Curriculum with independent reading, and some direct instruction in grammar, spelling, or phonics, schools can provide an inexpensive and innovative literature, language arts, and writing curriculum that is coordinated throughout the elementary school years.

The number of each series corresponds to its recommended grade level. Teachers might want to use an earlier series to accommodate less-able readers, but it is not necessary to adopt a higher series for better readers; the selections will present sufficient challenge for the best readers at each level. Two semesters of readings are available for Series 2-6; one semester of readings is available for Series 7-9.

The Curriculum for grade two serves as a transition between the Read-Aloud program and the Curriculum for the remaining elementary grades. Students using Series 2 follow the basic Read-Aloud sequence of two readings in class and one at home with discussion of open-ended questions printed in the margin of their books. Dramatizations and interpretive drawing activities are still offered, but increasing emphasis is placed upon interpretive discussion and individual writing. Students using Series 2 begin to participate in Shared Inquiry Discussion.

Junior Great Books Series 3 introduces Text Openers and Directed Notes, and makes Interpreting Words a regular part of each unit. With these additions, the Curriculum's basic structure—which continues through high school—is established.

Beginning in Series 5, the Curriculum introduces students to the shared inquiry method through a preface in their books, which explicitly addresses topics such as active reading, taking notes, listening and responding to fellow participants, the rules of Shared Inquiry Discussion, and writing interpretive questions.

The Junior Great Books Reading, Writing, and Discussion Sequence for Grades 2-9

SESSION 1

- Text Opener or answering a prereading question*
- First reading of the story (can be read aloud by the teacher)
- Sharing Questions

SESSION 2

- Second reading of the story (by students) in conjunction with Directed Notes**

SESSION 3

- Interpreting Words

SESSION 4

- Shared Inquiry Discussion

SESSION 5

- Creative and expository writing

  * Not done in Series 2

  ** In Series 2, students hear the story read aloud three times and discuss questions printed in the margin of their books.

First Semester

THE HAPPY LION   *Louise Fatio*

THE TALE OF SQUIRREL NUTKIN   *Beatrix Potter*

HOW THE CAMEL GOT HIS HUMP   *Rudyard Kipling*

KANGA AND BABY ROO COME TO THE FOREST,
AND PIGLET HAS A BATH
(from WINNIE-THE-POOH)   *A. A. Milne*

ARAP SANG AND THE CRANES
African folktale as told by Humphrey Harman

BLUE MOOSE   *Daniel Manus Pinkwater*

ANANCY AND DOG AND PUSS AND FRIENDSHIP
West Indian folktale as told by James Berry

JACK AND THE BEANSTALK
English folktale as told by Joseph Jacobs

THE MAGIC LISTENING CAP
Japanese folktale as told by Yoshiko Uchida

THE JACKAL AND THE PARTRIDGE
Punjabi folktale as told by Flora Annie Steel

NAIL SOUP   *Swedish folktale as told by Linda Rahm*

THE APPLE OF CONTENTMENT   *Howard Pyle*

Second Semester

THE RED BALLOON   *Albert Lamorisse*

THE OTHER SIDE OF THE HILL   *Elizabeth Coatsworth*

THE EMPEROR'S NEW CLOTHES
Hans Christian Andersen

HOW THE ELEPHANT BECAME   *Ted Hughes*

ANANSI'S FISHING EXPEDITION
West African folktale as told by Harold Courlander and George Herzog

THE VELVETEEN RABBIT   *Margery Williams*

THE TERRIBLE LEAK   *Japanese folktale as told by Yoshiko Uchida*

THE SINGING TORTOISE
West African folktale as told by Harold Courlander and George Herzog

THREE BOYS WITH JUGS OF MOLASSES
AND SECRET AMBITIONS   *Carl Sandburg*

CINDERELLA   *Charles Perrault*

THE MOUSE'S BRIDE   *Indian folktale as told by Lucia Turnbull*

HOW COYOTE STOLE THE SUN
Native American folktale as told by Jane Louise Curry

Series 2 materials (TWO SEMESTERS):

The student book for each semester contains twelve selections. Teacher's Editions for each semester include full instructions for conducting the Curriculum, an annotated student text, suggested interpretive questions for Shared Inquiry Discussion, and black-and-white activity page masters.

SERIES 3

First Semester

THE MASTER CAT   *Charles Perrault*

THE FISHERMAN AND HIS WIFE
Brothers Grimm, translated by Lucy Crane

THE LITTLE DAUGHTER OF THE SNOW
Russian folktale as told by Arthur Ransome

THE UGLY DUCKLING   *Hans Christian Andersen*

THE MONSTER WHO GREW SMALL   *Joan Grant*

THE LITTLE HUMPBACKED HORSE
Russian folktale as told by Post Wheeler

OOKA AND THE HONEST THIEF
Japanese folktale as told by I. G. Edmonds

THE BRAVE LITTLE TAILOR
Brothers Grimm, translated by Ralph Manheim

JEAN LABADIE'S BIG BLACK DOG
French-Canadian folktale as told by Natalie Savage Carlson

CAPORUSHES   *English folktale as told by Flora Annie Steel*

IT'S ALL THE FAULT OF ADAM
Nigerian folktale as told by Barbara Walker

TWO WISE CHILDREN   *Robert Graves*

Second Semester

THE BLACK HEART OF INDRI   *Dorothy Hoge*

THE GREEN MAN   *Gail E. Haley*

THE MOUSEWIFE   *Rumer Godden*

THE FIRE ON THE MOUNTAIN
Ethiopian folktale as told by Harold Courlander and Wolf Leslau

WOMAN'S WIT   *Howard Pyle*

THE MAN WHOSE TRADE WAS TRICKS
Georgian folktale as told by George and Helen Papashvily

HOW THE TORTOISE BECAME   *Ted Hughes*

TOM-TIT-TOT   *English folktale as told by Flora Annie Steel*

THE SNOWMAN   *Hans Christian Andersen*

ELLEN'S LION   *Crockett Johnson*

THE RIVER BANK
(from THE WIND IN THE WILLOWS)   *Kenneth Grahame*

THE OPEN ROAD
(from THE WIND IN THE WILLOWS)   *Kenneth Grahame*

SERIES 4

First Semester

THANK YOU, M'AM   *Langston Hughes*

THE WATER-HORSE OF BARRA
Scottish folktale as told by Winifred Finlay

THE STORY OF WANG LI   *Elizabeth Coatsworth*

THE ELEPHANT'S CHILD   *Rudyard Kipling*

VASILISSA THE BEAUTIFUL
Russian folktale as told by Post Wheeler

CEDRIC   *Tove Jansson*

FRESH   *Philippa Pearce*

THE ENCHANTED STICKS   *Steven J. Myers*

WISDOM'S WAGES AND FOLLY'S PAY
Howard Pyle

MR. SINGER'S NICKNAMES   *James Krüss*

ALICE'S ADVENTURES IN WONDERLAND
(SELECTION)   *Lewis Carroll*

Second Semester

THUNDER, ELEPHANT, AND DOROBO
African folktale as told by Humphrey Harman

THE MAN WITH THE WEN
Japanese folktale as told by Idries Shah

ALI BABA AND THE FORTY THIEVES
(from THE ARABIAN NIGHTS)

THE GOLDFISH   *Eleanor Farjeon*

BEAUTY AND THE BEAST   *Madame de Villeneuve*

PROT AND KROT   *Polish folktale as told by Agnes Szudek*

THE HEMULEN WHO LOVED SILENCE
Tove Jansson

THE DEVOTED FRIEND   *Oscar Wilde*

THE DANCING PRINCESSES   *Walter de la Mare*

ALLAH WILL PROVIDE
North African folktale as told by Robert Gilstrap and Irene Estabrook

MR. TOAD
(from THE WIND IN THE WILLOWS)   *Kenneth Grahame*

THE FURTHER ADVENTURES OF TOAD
(from THE WIND IN THE WILLOWS)   *Kenneth Grahame*

SERIES 5

First Semester

CHARLES *Shirley Jackson*

GHOST CAT *Donna Hill*

TURQUOISE HORSE *Gerald Hausman*

MAURICE'S ROOM *Paula Fox*

BARBIE *Gary Soto*

LENNY'S RED-LETTER DAY *Bernard Ashley*

THE PRINCE AND THE GOOSE GIRL *Elinor Mordaunt*

TRAMP *Malcolm Carrick*

ALBERIC THE WISE *Norton Juster*

PODHU AND ARUWA
African folktale as told by Humphrey Harman

THE INVISIBLE CHILD *Tove Jansson*

THE BAT-POET *Randall Jarrell*

Second Semester

A GAME OF CATCH *Richard Wilbur*

THE TALE OF THE THREE STORYTELLERS
James Krüss

SPIT NOLAN *Bill Naughton*

THE QUEEN'S CARE *Elizabeth Jamison Hodges*

LUCKY BOY *Philippa Pearce*

THE SECRET OF THE HATTIFATTENERS
Tove Jansson

THE HAPPY PRINCE *Oscar Wilde*

KADDO'S WALL
West African folktale as told by Harold Courlander and George Herzog

DITA'S STORY *Mary Q. Steele*

OLIVER HYDE'S DISHCLOTH CONCERT
Richard Kennedy

MOWGLI'S BROTHERS
(from THE JUNGLE BOOKS) *Rudyard Kipling*

"TIGER-TIGER!"
(from THE JUNGLE BOOKS) *Rudyard Kipling*

SERIES 6

First Semester

THROUGH THE TUNNEL *Doris Lessing*

RAYMOND'S RUN *Toni Cade Bambara*

MY GREATEST AMBITION *Morris Lurie*

A LIKELY PLACE *Paula Fox*

THE MYSTERIES OF THE CABALA *Isaac Bashevis Singer*

BAD CHARACTERS *Jean Stafford*

CHURA AND MARWE *African folktale as told by Humphrey Harman*

SUPERSTITIONS *Mary La Chapelle*

THE LAST GREAT SNAKE *Mary Q. Steele*

GASTON *William Saroyan*

SOUMCHI *Amos Oz*

Second Semester

THE VELDT *Ray Bradbury*

THE WHITE UMBRELLA *Gish Jen*

THE PARSLEY GARDEN *William Saroyan*

THE SECRET OF THE YELLOW HOUSE *Anatoly Aleksin*

AS THE NIGHT THE DAY *Abioseh Nicol*

THE SUMMER BOOK *Tove Jansson*

THE ALLIGATORS *John Updike*

TWEEDLEDUM AND TWEEDLEDEE
(from THROUGH THE LOOKING-GLASS) *Lewis Carroll*

THE MAGIC JACKET *Walter de la Mare*

PROPS FOR FAITH *Ursula Hegi*

LETTING IN THE JUNGLE
(from THE JUNGLE BOOKS) *Rudyard Kipling*

THE SPRING RUNNING
(from THE JUNGLE BOOKS) *Rudyard Kipling*

Series 3-6 materials (TWO SEMESTERS):

For each semester there is a student book of twelve selections, and a student activity book. Schools can purchase
one activity book for each student, or a single copy for use as a black-and-white duplicating master. Teacher's Editions
for each semester include full instructions for conducting the Curriculum, an annotated student text, and suggested
interpretive questions for Shared Inquiry Discussion.

SERIES 7

HARRISON BERGERON   *Kurt Vonnegut, Jr.*

I JUST KEPT ON SMILING   *Simon Burt*

AT HER FATHER'S AND HER MOTHER'S PLACE
Natalya Baranskaya

THE WHITE CIRCLE   *John Bell Clayton*

THE ZODIACS   *Jay Neugeboren*

END OF THE GAME   *Julio Cortázar*

THE CAT AND THE COFFEE DRINKERS   *Max Steele*

ANNE FRANK: THE DIARY OF A YOUNG GIRL
(SELECTION)

THE SECRET LION   *Alberto Alvaro Ríos*

DAY OF THE BUTTERFLY   *Alice Munro*

A CHRISTMAS CAROL   *Charles Dickens*

SERIES 8

SUCKER   *Carson McCullers*

THE SUMMER OF THE BEAUTIFUL WHITE HORSE
William Saroyan

RULES OF THE GAME
(from THE JOY LUCK CLUB)   *Amy Tan*

THE DESTRUCTORS   *Graham Greene*

THE WATCH   *Ivan Turgenev*

APPROXIMATIONS   *Mona Simpson*

THE GRIFFIN AND THE MINOR CANON
Frank R. Stockton

STAR FOOD   *Ethan Canin*

WINTER
(from THE WINTER ROOM)   *Gary Paulsen*

HIGH SCHOOL GRADUATION
(from I KNOW WHY THE CAGED BIRD SINGS)   *Maya Angelou*

ADVENTURES OF HUCKLEBERRY FINN
(SELECTION)   *Mark Twain*

SERIES 9

MIRIAM   *Truman Capote*

ZOO ISLAND   *Tomás Rivera*

AT THE PITT-RIVERS   *Penelope Lively*

NEW AFRICAN
(from SARAH PHILLIPS)   *Andrea Lee*

SPONONO   *Alan Paton*

BOBBY'S ROOM   *Douglas Dunn*

A BIRD IN THE HOUSE   *Margaret Laurence*

THE STRANGE CASE OF DR. JEKYLL AND MR. HYDE
Robert Louis Stevenson

THE LITTLE COUSINS   *Peter Taylor*

THE IDEALIST   *Frank O'Connor*

THE TIME MACHINE   *H. G. Wells*

Series 7-9 materials (ONE SEMESTER):

Each student book contains twelve selections. Leader's Guides include full instructions for conducting the Curriculum, and, for each selection, a choice of prereading questions, a Directed Notes source, an Interpreting Words activity, suggested interpretive questions for Shared Inquiry Discussion, and a choice of Writing After Discussion questions.

Since students are encouraged to read actively by taking notes in their books, we urge that student books for all Junior Great Books series be used as consumables. Teacher's Editions are required for implementing the full Curriculum and are strongly recommended for volunteer and teacher-led pull-out programs.

Introduction to Great Books (Grades 10-12)

Introduction to Great Books involves students in reading some of the finest classic and modern authors and in thinking reflectively about the questions of enduring significance they raise. Each series includes brief works of nonfiction—essays in philosophy, history, economics, sociology, and psychology—as well as short stories and plays. The program stresses writing as an integral part of students' ongoing, personal interaction with the text.

Introduction to Great Books is a flexible program in which the full complement of interpretive activities for each selection can be conducted in four or five class sessions, or in as little as two—with the prereading and post-discussion writing, and the reading and note taking done as homework. The first classroom period then focuses on the sharing of questions, notes, and preliminary ideas; the second is devoted to Shared Inquiry Discussion.

The timelessness and universality of the selections and the openness of the shared inquiry method make Introduction to Great Books appropriate for a variety of students, including average and above-average readers in high school, and freshmen and sophomores in college. In addition, adults starting a Great Books group can use the program to familiarize themselves with the shared inquiry method before moving on to the Great Books Reading and Discussion Program.

**The Introduction to Great Books
Reading, Writing, and Discussion Sequence**

SESSION 1

· Answering a prereading question

· First reading of the selection, orally by teacher or by students

· Sharing students' questions

SESSION 2

· Second reading of the selection in conjunction with
     Directed Notes

SESSION 3

· Vocabulary work or preparing passage for textual analysis,
     or writing own interpretive questions

SESSION 4

· Shared Inquiry Discussion

SESSION 5

· Creative and expository writing

FIRST SERIES

WHY WAR?   *Sigmund Freud*

THE MELIAN DIALOGUE   *Thucydides*

THE SOCIAL ME   *William James*

ROTHSCHILD'S FIDDLE   *Anton Chekhov*

CONCERNING THE DIVISION OF LABOR   *Adam Smith*

CHELKASH   *Maxim Gorky*

HOW AN ARISTOCRACY MAY BE CREATED
BY INDUSTRY   *Alexis de Tocqueville*

OBSERVATION AND EXPERIMENT   *Claude Bernard*

EVERYTHING THAT RISES MUST CONVERGE
Flannery O'Connor

AN ESSAY IN AESTHETICS   *Roger Fry*

AN OUTPOST OF PROGRESS   *Joseph Conrad*

ON STUDYING   *José Ortega y Gasset*

SECOND SERIES

POLITICS   *Aristotle*

OF COMMONWEALTH   *Thomas Hobbes*

BARN BURNING   *William Faulkner*

OF CIVIL GOVERNMENT   *John Locke*

IN EXILE   *Anton Chekhov*

THE DECLARATION OF INDEPENDENCE

EQUALITY
Isaiah Berlin

SORROW-ACRE   *Isak Dinesen*

WHY AMERICANS ARE OFTEN SO RESTLESS
Alexis de Tocqueville

AFTER THE BALL   *Leo Tolstoy*

HABIT   *William James*

THE OVERCOAT   *Nikolai Gogol*

THIRD SERIES

ON HAPPINESS   *Aristotle*

HABITS AND WILL   *John Dewey*

HAPPINESS   *Mary Lavin*

CRITO   *Plato*

ON LIBERTY   *John Stuart Mill*

CONSCIENCE   *Immanuel Kant*

A HUNGER ARTIST   *Franz Kafka*

OF THE LIMITS OF GOVERNMENT   *John Locke*

ANTIGONE   *Sophocles*

WHY GREAT REVOLUTIONS WILL BECOME RARE
Alexis de Tocqueville

A ROOM OF ONE'S OWN   *Virginia Woolf*

IN DREAMS BEGIN RESPONSIBILITIES
Delmore Schwartz

Introduction to Great Books materials:

The student book for each of the three series contains twelve selections, accompanied by essays and exercises on the shared inquiry method. Leader's Guides contain full instructions for conducting the Curriculum, and, for each selection, choices of prereading questions, Directed Notes sources, suggested interpretive questions for Shared Inquiry Discussion, and Post-Discussion Writing questions.

Since students are encouraged to read actively by taking notes in their books, we urge that students use the Introduction to Great Books texts as consumables.

5

GREAT BOOKS PROGRAMS
IN THE CLASSROOM AND
THE COMMUNITY

To achieve its educational goals, a Junior Great Books program should be consistent and ongoing. Enlisting the support of parents and members of the community is the best way to build effective programs in which students can develop the attitudes and skills that will make them accomplished readers. Great Books discussion groups for adults provide a unique opportunity for continuing self-education and can solidify support for Junior Great Books programs in the community.

VOLUNTEER-LED AND PULL-OUT PROGRAMS
School-based Junior Great Books programs have a long tradition of parental involvement. For over thirty years, parents have shared their love of reading with children by organizing Junior Great Books programs in their schools and becoming discussion leaders themselves. Now, with the availability of the new Junior Great Books Curriculum, volunteers have many more opportunities to contribute to their children's education.

The Junior Great Books Curriculum invites collaboration between teachers and volunteers. If yours is a whole-class program, trained volunteers can lead half the class in Shared Inquiry Discussion while the teacher leads the other half. This will serve to make discussion more intimate and productive, with each student having more chances to participate. Volunteers can also help lead other Curriculum activities. Because each Curriculum activity focuses on the interpretation of a Junior Great Books selection, volunteers experienced in leading Shared Inquiry Discussion will be well prepared to lead these effectively.

If yours is a once-a-week pull-out program, you can enrich your discussions by using Curriculum activities. The new Curriculum reinforces the Junior Great Books process of active reading—reading twice, taking notes, and formulating interpretive questions—which leaders have always encouraged students to follow. The more activities students participate in, the more they will benefit from Shared Inquiry Discussion.

Ask your students' teacher to do the first reading in class. (All students will enjoy hearing the stories read aloud, whether or not they participate in the program.) To encourage students to complete a thoughtful second reading of a selection, you can assign the Directed Notes when you assign each story; then begin your meetings with a brief sharing of notes. To emphasize the connection between writing and thinking, ask the classroom teacher to assign some activity pages—especially the creative writing and essays—as independent language arts work or as homework. These simple additions will build a firmer commitment to your program, and will make your discussions more lively and focused. You might also expand your program to meet twice a week so that you can lead some of the Curriculum activities yourself. Volunteer leaders are encouraged to use the Curriculum's Teacher's Editions and Leader's Guides to improve the quality of their programs.

Finally, volunteers can be invaluable in building schoolwide implementation of the Junior Great Books Curriculum. They can organize meetings to inform parents of the benefits of the program and encourage their at-home support; they can also develop sources for outside funding. Volunteers can work toward expanding the grade levels at which Junior Great Books is offered and be instrumental in converting pull-out programs to full in-class programs that can include a wider range of students.

Volunteers can be active in Junior Great Books in any of its various settings. Schools currently use Junior Great Books in classes as part of the regular reading/language arts curriculum, with groups of gifted students, and with disadvantaged students in an accelerated curriculum. In addition, many schools, libraries, and community centers offer Junior Great Books as an extracurricular program.

A Note to Read-Aloud Program Users

The Read-Aloud program should not be implemented as a pull-out program. Kindergarten and first grade students cannot prepare for interpretive discussion on their own, as older children can. To arrive at thoughtful interpretations, young children need the structure of the repeated readings as well as the interpretive activities which are designed to build on each other and provide prereaders with concrete help in exploring literature. Through interpretive art, dramatizations, group composition, and above all, sharing ideas aloud, young students can begin to internalize the process of thoughtful reading that they will practice in the Junior Great Books program for older grades. Of course, parents play a vital role in the Read-Aloud program when they read aloud and discuss G.B.'s Questions with their children, and help them to write down their favorite questions and new vocabulary words. And trained volunteers can still help in the classroom by leading Sharing Questions Discussion and any of the other Read-Aloud activities.

MAINTAINING A STRONG JUNIOR GREAT BOOKS PROGRAM

Maintaining a Junior Great Books program involves recruiting leaders, overseeing training and ongoing leader development, arranging for funding, and cultivating parental and community support. One trained leader in your school can serve as the Junior Great Books coordinator and be responsible for these tasks. Many school systems have a district-level Junior Great Books coordinator as well.

The Great Books Foundation can help you implement your Junior Great Books program. Call the Foundation and ask the regional coordinator for your state to answer your questions about the Junior Great Books Curriculum and help you schedule Basic Leader Training Courses and Curriculum training. Your regional coordinator can also suggest possible sources of outside funding, refer you to other schools that use Junior Great Books, and keep you informed about new materials as they become available.

Funding for Junior Great Books programs can be obtained in a variety of ways. Common funding sources are district and school improvement funds, PTA/PTO special projects, grants from corporations or foundations, state and federal categorical program funds, and student purchases. Your school or district Junior Great Books coordinator can serve as a liaison to potential funders.

Involving parents and making them aware of the special nature of Junior Great Books is one of the best ways to establish an effective program. Your school's coordinator or other spokesperson can make a presentation at PTA/PTO meetings to inform parents about the program and to encourage them to volunteer in the classroom. Teachers of Read-Aloud and second-grade groups might want to host an informal gathering to let parents know about their role in working with their child at home. The Teacher's Editions for the Junior program offer specific guidance, including sample letters to parents to help schools solidify parental participation and support.

Continuing leader development is the key to the most successful Junior Great Books programs. During the school year, leaders can help each other by scheduling regular meetings in order to share ideas, prepare for Shared Inquiry Discussion, and coach each other. The Foundation's newsletter, *Leader Notes,* features advice for improving discussions, articles about Junior Great Books authors and illustrators, profiles of successful programs, and a forum for leaders' questions and comments. Subscriptions cost $4.50 per year. Leaders can also develop their skills by taking the Foundation's Curriculum training.

THE GREAT BOOKS READING AND DISCUSSION PROGRAM FOR ADULTS

The Great Books Reading and Discussion Program introduces adult participants to substantial works of literature and philosophy. Group members enjoy both intellectual collaboration and the opportunity to reflect on their own lives and convictions in light of ideas from major thinkers. Many teachers and parents find that participating in a Great Books program themselves is an excellent way to support their children's Junior Great Books programs.

Participants in the program typically meet once a month for a one- or two-hour discussion. The setting is informal, such as a participant's home, a public library, or a church or school. They read, take notes, and prepare for discussion independently, following the procedure outlined in this manual. Frequently, two leaders are responsible for each discussion; ideally, they meet to discuss the selection (see p. 43, "Preparing with a Colleague or Co-leader"). Great Books groups may have permanent leaders or several leader-participants who take turns leading discussion. Occasionally, the whole group takes the Basic Leader Training Course, so that the responsibility for leading can be shared broadly, and all participants will understand more thoroughly the nature of the interpretive process.

The Great Books Reading and Discussion Program, with its stress on close reading, interpretation, and critical thinking in discussion, may be used in college courses that emphasize the development of reading, thinking, writing, and oral communication skills. Examples include freshman composition; an introductory course in the humanities, literature, or philosophy; and a freshman or senior seminar or honors course.

The program's shared inquiry method and emphasis on direct involvement with a text also makes it suitable for continuing education and nondegree programs stressing personal development. In addition, colleges, universities, and corporations have used Great Books in voluntary staff-development programs in order to promote intellectual and professional growth.

Reader Aids for the Great Books Reading and Discussion Program offer advice to participants about reading, taking notes, and writing their own questions on selections. They also include interpretive and evaluative questions for each selection in a series.

INFORMATION FOR SCHOOL ADMINISTRATORS

From kindergarten through grade twelve, the Junior Great Books Curriculum provides intensive work in constructing meaning from excellent literature. It fulfills the core reading/language arts objectives of critical thinking, reading comprehension, enjoyment of literature, oral communication, and writing. Because students in the Curriculum contribute freely at their own level of understanding, students of widely varying abilities can be involved. Gifted students thrive on the excellent literature and the concentration on sustained thinking; disadvantaged students gain higher-order skills from the Curriculum's emphasis on oral sharing of ideas and individualized attention.

Junior Great Books Curriculum Objectives

Higher-level language and thinking skills are acquired in conjunction with one another through the Curriculum's interpretive reading and writing activities and Shared Inquiry Discussion. We describe these skills separately here so that you may more easily consider them as you plan lessons and work with your students.

Reading

Reading skills are exercised at every stage of the shared inquiry process. Participants practice oral and silent reading, expand their vocabularies, and develop reading comprehension through activities such as taking and sharing notes, posing questions, textual analysis, and Shared Inquiry Discussion.

Deriving word meanings from context. This occurs as students explain the meaning of those passages they cite as evidence and, in many cases, as they answer the leader's interpretive questions.

Recalling details. Participants recall and often locate details in the text when they cite evidence from the selection to support their answer to an interpretive question.

Organizing details (time sequence, cause and effect). Students mentally arrange details in logical order as they master the facts of the selection and compare the evidence cited to support different opinions. The leader prompts students to organize details and to explain how they have done so by asking them to clarify and support their positions.

Drawing inferences. Answering factual, interpretive, and evaluative questions involves drawing inferences from the details in the selection. Follow-up questions that ask students to clarify their ideas often lead students to explain the inferences they have drawn.

Recognizing tone and point of view. Students' and leaders' interpretive questions frequently focus on the tone and point of view of particular passages or of a whole selection. Follow-up questions that ask students how they would read specific passages or how they reconcile various facts in the text usually require students to consider the author's attitude toward the characters and, in some cases, the reader.

Understanding characters. The motivation of characters is probably the most common source of students' and leaders' interpretive questions about stories; discussions frequently center on why characters in stories act as they do.

Finding the main idea of a passage. In writing interpretive questions, students find the main idea not only in one paragraph but in several paragraphs, and sometimes juxtapose different central ideas to present a problem of meaning in the selection. In Shared Inquiry Discussion, the leader guides students in finding the main idea and explaining how they found it, through textual analysis and follow-up questions asking why a passage was cited as evidence.

Drawing conclusions; finding the main idea of the text as a whole. Answering basic questions in Shared Inquiry Discussion involves finding and weighing possible "main ideas" for the whole selection. Students also explore comprehensive interpretive issues and major themes through Directed Notes and Interpreting Words activities, and by writing their own questions. In Writing After Discussion activities, students consolidate their ideas and draw their own conclusions about the meaning of the work.

Listening

Participation in the Curriculum's interpretive activities and in Shared Inquiry Discussion requires students to listen and respond to the leader's questions, as well as to the statements of their classmates. The leader models listening skills by paying close attention to participants' comments, noting their ideas on a seating chart, and posing questions in direct response to what participants say. The leader also encourages active listening and a cooperative attitude by asking questions that encourage participants to respond to each other's statements and to assist one another in recalling facts and explaining opinions.

Speaking

The Curriculum's interpretive activities and Shared Inquiry Discussion require students to present opinions, explain reasons for an inference or a conclusion, use persuasion, recite facts, recount others' opinions, and read aloud. In Shared Inquiry Discussion, the leader helps students achieve more coherent, varied, and complex oral expression by slowing the pace of discussion, encouraging participants to speak directly to each other, and asking thoughtful follow-up questions. By showing respect for and interest in all students' ideas, the leader helps participants learn to offer opposing viewpoints firmly but politely, and to maintain an orderly discourse.

Thinking

Consecutive, reflective thinking is called upon throughout shared inquiry as students explain their opinions and the evidence supporting them orally and in writing. In the interpretive activities and Shared Inquiry Discussion, students comment on others' statements, try to use evidence brought up by others, and modify their own thinking to make use of the ideas they hear.

Problem solving. Answering an interpretive question, orally or in writing, involves recognizing the problem that it poses and generating an original idea to resolve that problem.

Argument. In supporting an answer to an interpretive question, a student articulates and clarifies the opinion, explains the reasons behind it, and offers logical support in the form of evidence from the selection. Often, the participant must respond to points of view already stated and evidence already brought forward by classmates.

Critical thinking; analysis. To give an opinion on statements made by classmates, a student must analyze the arguments, assessing their logic and the evidence offered to support them.

Synthesis. Answering a basic question during Shared Inquiry Discussion involves bringing together many facts and inferences about a selection to form a single coherent statement. At the close of Shared Inquiry Discussion, students elaborate on their own initial opinions by accommodating ideas and evidence cited by other participants and reconciling or choosing among conflicting lines of thought.

CRITERIA FOR CHOOSING THE JUNIOR GREAT BOOKS SELECTIONS

The literature that is the basis of the Junior Great Books Curriculum is carefully chosen to support the interpretive work of leaders and participants in shared inquiry learning. It is this unique focus on interpretation that determines the following four criteria.

Selections must be able to support extended interpretive discussion. Because students in the Junior Great Books Curriculum participate in a collaborative search for meaning in a work, our primary criterion is that selections must invite and support a number of interpretations. Only selections that are sufficiently rich in ideas, and in which the author's meaning is not explicit, raise the interpretive questions necessary for sustained shared inquiry. And only well-crafted selections, works that are thematically complex and cohesive, suggest real answers—that is, interpretations that can be supported with evidence from the text rather than merely being a matter of personal opinion or free association.

Every piece of literature requires interpretation to some degree, but not all works lend themselves to extended interpretive analysis. The fact that a work is a "classic" is no guarantee that it can support shared inquiry. It may be beautifully written and uplifting—something that every young person should have the opportunity to experience—but if its meaning and intention are transparent to the individual reader, it cannot reward the sustained intellectual focus of the Curriculum's interpretive activities and Shared Inquiry Discussion. For example, not all of Rudyard Kipling's stories in *The Jungle Books* are appropriate for the Junior Great Books series. Our selections ("Mowgli's Brothers," "Tiger-Tiger!" "Letting in the Jungle," and "The Spring Running") support interpretive discussion, but the perennial favorite, "Rikki-Tikki-Tavi," does not—despite the fact that all these memorable tales touch upon many of the same themes.

"Rikki-Tikki-Tavi," which tells how a brave young mongoose protects a human household from two menacing cobras, is an inspiring tale of animal heroism. It is a satisfying story in which evil is defeated and resourcefulness and courage are rewarded. But the motives of the characters are clear; the story's outcome raises no particular questions or problems of understanding in the reader's mind. There is nothing paradoxical or curious about the story that invites further reflection or demands explanation.

The Mowgli stories, however, are problematic. Here we are led more deeply into themes of belonging and isolation, and uncertainty about finding one's proper place. The Junior Great Books selections tell how the boy Mowgli grows up a member of the Seeonee wolf pack, only to be cast out by his "brothers" as he approaches adulthood. Because it is not clear why Mowgli is rejected, both by the wolves whom he loves and by the people of the village (presumably his proper home), the stories present interpretive questions that can be addressed through shared inquiry. By focusing on such questions, students are able to go beyond reading the Mowgli stories merely as adventure. They are able to appreciate Kipling's subtle portrayal of profound human forces and concerns, and to understand and gain insight from the character of Mowgli, who grows up noble and strong despite being separated from his own kind.

Selections must raise genuine questions for adults as well as students. Junior Great Books selections must appeal to adults since their curiosity about what a work of literature has to say is the driving force behind shared inquiry. Providing selections that speak to both leaders and students helps ensure that shared inquiry will be a collaborative effort. In preparing to lead the Curriculum's activities and Shared Inquiry Discussion, leaders go through the same kind of intensive interaction with the text that they want to encourage in their students: they read the selection at least twice, note whatever they find puzzling or thought-provoking, and write interpretive questions that express their own search for meaning in the work. In so doing, leaders serve as a model of an active and involved partner in shared inquiry; they engender in young people the expectations that they can find answers within themselves, and take responsibility for their own learning.

In the Read-Aloud program, selections must not only support teachers' thoughtful engagement with the stories and poems, but also encourage parents' ready participation in the regularly scheduled at-home sessions. When parents read the selections aloud to their children with enthusiasm, and discuss the open-ended questions in the books with real interest, they communicate a vital message about the value and pleasure of reading for meaning.

But stories that meet this double requirement—that have the kind of universal, ageless themes and rich, lively language that engage both adults and youngsters—are rare. Factors disqualifying a selection range from the obvious— explicit sexual references, for example—to the subtle. A story in which the narrator recalls a childhood experience in order to address adult concerns, for instance, would be unsuitable for young readers. Or a story might be inappropriate because it is too ironic—too adult in tone or point of view.

Selections must be limited in length so that students can read each selection at least twice and work with it closely. Through concentrated work on a single text over a period of several days, students in the Junior Great Books Curriculum learn how to read closely—to examine details and draw connections—always with the purpose of working out answers to substantial questions of interpretation. Short stories and novellas are better suited than novels to this intensive work, which includes reading the selection twice, taking and sharing notes, concentrating on significant vocabulary, posing questions about the overall meaning of the story, and participating in thoughtful discussion.

In the Junior Great Books series, we have occasionally been able to include excerpts from full-length novels. This is the exception, however, since novels rarely yield excerpts that are self-contained. Nonfiction, on the other hand, often does. And so we are able to include in the Introduction to Great Books series short selections from works of philosophy, history, economics, sociology, and psychology.

Selections must be age-appropriate. When deciding in which series to place a selection, we give primary consideration to the appropriateness of its theme and style for a particular grade, rather than to standard assessments of reading levels. In all of the Junior Great Books series, including the Read-Aloud program, students encounter the original words of the author: no texts have been modified to meet a controlled vocabulary.

Deciding if a selection is appropriate for a certain age group requires judging whether its themes are presented on a level suited to the students' intellectual and emotional growth. In the primary grades, for instance, the folktales we publish are among the most popular—and most thought-provoking—selections in the entire Junior series. By presenting universal ideas in a manner that can touch the inexperienced mind of a child, folktales give expression to such childhood concerns as the need for self-control, as expressed in "The Fisherman and His Wife," and the struggle for independence, found in "Jack and the Beanstalk." Similarly, the modern children's stories included in the elementary grade series—such as those by Rumer Godden, Langston Hughes, and Paula Fox—treat themes that are particularly accessible for youngsters.

In the middle grades, although the magical and fantastic still has its appeal, students' tastes begin to change. They become drawn to stories that treat their concerns in more realistic contexts. Because most realistic fiction written for children neither supports shared inquiry nor holds real intellectual interest for adults, we must expand our search for selections to include works by authors who write for an adult audience. For example, "Raymond's Run" by Toni Cade Bambara was not written as a children's story, but it vividly captures a childhood experience—about family loyalty and competition in the larger world—in a manner that young people can understand and appreciate.

At the high school level, an even greater number of works written for adults are accessible to students. The classic drama, modern fiction, and short nonfiction selections published in the three Introduction to Great Books series have been chosen for their appeal to adolescents and young adults. For perhaps the first time, students explore the meaning of primary texts of philosophy, reflecting on such enduring questions as *How can society achieve justice?* and *Is there a "real me" apart from my social selves?*

Although we would like every selection to be equally popular with all Junior Great Books participants, we are aware that some of the works we publish may not immediately engage young readers. Nevertheless, we believe that the Curriculum's interpretive activities and Shared Inquiry Discussion enable students to overcome any initial difficulties and connect eagerly with the thought-provoking issues raised by the selections. Through Junior Great Books, leaders can guide students in broadening their tastes and ideas. It is the Foundation's conviction that if students are to develop the habits of inquiry and intellectual exchange essential to a lifetime of learning, then they must be given the opportunity to grapple with challenging literature—works rich in ideas that allow young readers to ask and seek answers to the question, "What does this mean?"

The search for new selections is ongoing. Even with the abundance of new children's books published each year, it is not easy to find selections that help us give young people the unique reading experience offered by Junior Great Books. All selections are tested by Foundation staff to see if they meet our primary criterion of discussability; many stories that initially look promising do not pass our rigorous review process.

To find new selections, we keep a close watch on new publications by screening national review periodicals, such as *Horn Book,* the *Bulletin of the Center for Children's Books,* and the American Library Association's *Booklist,* as well as international periodicals. Because we aim for ethnic diversity in our lists, we also seek out catalogs from small presses, such as Arte Publico Press and Howard University Press, for Hispanic-American, African-American, Asian-American, and Native American literature.

In addition, we look at the works in translation of outstanding international writers, such as James Krüss and Tove Jansson. We also have experts in children's literature from Africa, Australia, Europe, and Central and South America searching for selections not yet translated into English. And since much quality literature—especially children's—goes out of print very quickly, we comb libraries and used-book stores for promising works.

Periodically, we revise the Junior Great Books series. The decision to drop some selections from our lists and add others is based in part on information gathered from direct contact with teachers and administrators active in the program. Letters from leaders and our staff's own experience in leading Junior Great Books groups also provide useful information. But, most important, we depend on evaluations and questionnaires filled out by active leaders nationwide. Leaders are asked to rate each selection they have used on the basis of student appeal, discussibility, and age-appropriateness. Their answers help us determine not only which selections students enjoy reading initially, but also which stories "improve" after close analysis and discussion. Generally, we drop selections that do not have a high positive rating in all these areas.

It is vital for us to keep abreast of new authors and to stay sensitive to the shifting needs of our nation's schools, with the understanding that we can always improve the Junior Great Books series. In this effort, we invite your help.

APPENDIX A:

COURSE MATERIALS

STORIES

"The King of the Frogs"

"Jack and the Beanstalk"

"A Game of Catch"

"The Melian Dialogue"

EXERCISES

Building Your Answer in Shared Inquiry Discussion

Distinguishing Factual, Interpretive, and Evaluative Questions:

Exercise for "Jack and the Beanstalk"

Asking Follow-up Questions:

Exercise for "A Game of Catch"

THE KING OF THE FROGS

African folktale as told by Humphrey Harman

Have you ever been beside a lake in Africa at night and listened to the frogs? You haven't? Then you cannot imagine what the noise is like. And it's not just one kind of noise, it's several. Over there for instance are a thousand creaking doors that have never had their hinges oiled and someone opens and shuts them—and keeps on doing just that. Over *there* are a thousand fat men snoring and no one wakes them up. Then there are a thousand carpenters sawing planks and all the saws want a touch of grease, and a thousand little bells are being struck and a thousand corks are being pulled out of bottles.

Noise! You can hardly hear yourself think.

Then you go a little closer until you can just see the edge of the water and perhaps a reed or two and there is silence. Just the splash of a frog jumping into the water late because he was asleep and didn't hear you coming. Then nothing, and you can hear the whole world breathe.

There's a story about this.

Long ago the frogs did as they pleased and the result was dreadful. Not one of them would listen to what another said and they all shouted at once. Children wouldn't obey their parents and even wives wouldn't listen to their husbands, which is, indeed, something hardly to be understood. It was all noisy and untidy beyond bearing and nothing ever got done.

At last a wise, wise old frog called everyone to a meeting and, since he had a very fine voice and went on shouting for long enough, he managed to get them all there at once, for to tell you the truth they were pretty sick of living the way they did.

"Frogs!" said the old frog, puffing himself up. "We cannot go on like this. It's no sort of life for anyone and, anyway, when you see how all the other creatures live it makes one ashamed of being a frog. There is only one thing to do. We must get a king. When people have kings there is peace and order and everyone does as he is told."

"Agreed!" they all shouted and they stayed long enough to commission the old frog to see what he could do about getting them one, before everybody fell to quarreling and pushing and splashing and the meeting broke up in disorder. As usual.

Then the wise, wise old frog went to see the Great God Mmumi (you will say the two *m*'s correctly if you hum a little before you begin the word). Mmumi happened to be in charge of that part of the world.

He is a very slow god and usually gives people more than they bargain for. He agreed drowsily that the frogs needed a king and promised to do something about it. Then he went to sleep again.

So the frogs went on as usual, which was badly, until one day Mmumi woke up, remembered his promise, took a great green mossy boulder which had the rough shape of a gigantic frog and threw it into the water. SPLASH!

"There you are!" he shouted (it sounded like thunder). "There's your king. His name's Gogo and like me he doesn't want to be disturbed. Respect him and be satisfied."

The whole lake was shaken by Gogo's fall. The waves washed through the reeds and tore up the shore, and in the middle of a great cloud of mud Gogo settled on the bottom and the fat green waterweeds curled round and over him. He looked shocking.

The frogs were terrified and fled under stones and into dark corners and holes under the bank. Their long white legs streaked behind them as they swam. Parents found their children and husbands their wives and then settled down to explaining what had happened.

"This is our king," they said, "and a fine terrible one he seems, and from the splash he made not the sort to fool about with. Now all will be well and this scandalous behavior will stop."

And so it did, for a while.

But although Gogo had made such a wonderful first impression, as time passed they noticed that he never moved. He just sat quietly in the mud and stared in the same direction. Presently they began to get used to him, until finally some young, bold, bad frogs ventured to swim close to him and then one of them touched his nose.

And still Gogo said and did nothing.

"Bah! He's not a king!" they shouted. "He's not even a frog. He's just an old stone and couldn't hurt anyone." And they swam round him until they were dizzy and jumped all over his back and went away and spoke rudely about him to their elders.

At first none of the elders believed them. They had told their children Gogo was a king and a king he had to be, but soon it was impossible to deny that the children were right and then. . . . Well, the noise began again and things were as they had always been, only worse. Terrible!

The wise, wise old frog sighed and set out to see Mmumi again, who was not at all pleased at being woken a second time.

"All right!" he shouted in a passion. "*All right!* You aren't satisfied with the king I've given you. Is that the way it is? Very well, you shall have another and I hope you like him."

And the very next night he gave them Mamba the Crocodile.

Gogo had come to his people with a splash that shook the lake but Mamba slid into the water with only a whisper and left but one small ring spreading gently to show that he had come. Then he swam, silent as a shadow, lithe and long and secret, his jaws grinning like a trap. Gogo had never visited the people he had been given to rule but Mamba visited them often and suddenly, and whenever he met a subject the great jaws gaped and closed and often it was the last of that frog.

The frogs developed the greatest respect for their new king and lived quietly, looking over the backs of their heads as frogs can. Now and again at night they break out but they keep their ears open and if you go near the lake they shut up.

They think that it's Mamba coming to put a little order into them and they keep quiet.

JACK AND THE BEANSTALK

English folktale as told by Joseph Jacobs

There was once upon a time a poor widow who had an only son named Jack and a cow named Milky-white. And all they had to live on was the milk the cow gave every morning, which they carried to the market and sold. But one morning Milky-white gave no milk and they didn't know what to do.

"What shall we do, what shall we do?" said the widow, wringing her hands.

"Cheer up, mother, I'll go and get work somewhere," said Jack.

"We've tried that before, and nobody would take you," said his mother. "We must sell Milky-white and with the money start a shop or something."

"All right, mother," says Jack. "It's market day today, and I'll soon sell Milky-white, and then we'll see what we can do."

So he took the cow's halter in his hand, and off he started. He hadn't gone far when he met a funny-looking old man who said to him: "Good morning, Jack."

"Good morning to you," said Jack, and wondered how he knew his name.

"Well, Jack, and where are you off to?" said the man.

"I'm going to market to sell our cow here."

"Oh, you look the proper sort of chap to sell cows," said the man. "I wonder if you know how many beans make five."

"Two in each hand and one in your mouth," says Jack, as sharp as a needle.

"Right you are," says the man. "And here they are, the very beans themselves," he went on, pulling out of his pocket a number of strange-looking beans. "As you are so sharp," says he, "I don't mind doing a swap with you—your cow for these beans."

"Go along," says Jack. "Wouldn't you like it?"

"Ah! you don't know what these beans are," said the man. "If you plant them overnight, by morning they grow right up to the sky."

"Really?" says Jack. "You don't say so."

"Yes, that is so, and if it doesn't turn out to be true you can have your cow back."

"Right," says Jack, and hands him over Milky-white's halter and pockets the beans.

Back goes Jack home, and as he hadn't gone very far it wasn't dusk by the time he got to his door.

"Back already, Jack?" said his mother. "I see you haven't got Milky-white, so you've sold her. How much did you get for her?"

"You'll never guess, mother," says Jack.

"No, you don't say so. Good boy! Five pounds, ten, fifteen, no, it can't be twenty."

"I told you you couldn't guess. What do you say to these beans; they're magical, plant them overnight and—"

"What!" says Jack's mother. "Have you been such a fool, such a dolt, such an idiot, as to give away my Milky-white, the best milker in the parish, and prime beef to boot, for a set of paltry beans? Take that! Take that! Take that! And as for your precious beans, here they go out of the window. And now off with you to bed. Not a sip shall you drink, and not a bit shall you swallow this very night."

So Jack went upstairs to his little room in the attic, and sad and sorry he was, to be sure, as much for his mother's sake as for the loss of his supper.

At last he dropped off to sleep.

When he woke up, the room looked so funny. The sun was shining into part of it, and yet all the rest was quite dark and shady. So Jack jumped up and dressed himself and went to the window. And what do you think he saw? Why, the beans his mother had thrown out of the window into the garden had sprung up into a big beanstalk which went up and up and up till it reached the sky. So the man spoke truth after all.

The beanstalk grew up quite close past Jack's window, so all he had to do was to open it and give a jump onto the beanstalk, which ran up just like a big ladder. So Jack climbed, and he climbed and he climbed and he climbed and he climbed and he climbed and he climbed till at last he reached the sky. And when he got there he found a long broad road going as straight as a dart. So he walked along and he walked along and he walked along till he came to a great big tall house, and on the doorstep there was a great big tall woman.

"Good morning, mum," says Jack, quite polite-like. "Could you be so kind as to give me some breakfast?" For he hadn't had anything to eat, you know, the night before and was as hungry as a hunter.

"It's breakfast you want, is it?" says the great big tall woman. "It's breakfast you'll be if you don't move off from here. My man is an ogre and there's nothing he likes better than boys broiled on toast. You'd better be moving on or he'll soon be coming."

"Oh! please mum, do give me something to eat, mum. I've had nothing to eat since yesterday morning, really and truly, mum," says Jack. "I may as well be broiled as die of hunger."

Well, the ogre's wife was not half so bad after all. So she took Jack into the kitchen and gave him a chunk of bread and cheese and a jug of milk. But Jack hadn't half finished these when thump! thump! thump! the whole house began to tremble with the noise of someone coming.

"Goodness gracious me! It's my old man," said the ogre's wife. "What on earth shall I do? Come along quick and jump in here." And she bundled Jack into the oven just as the ogre came in.

He was a big one, to be sure. At his belt he had three calves strung up by the heels, and he unhooked them and threw them down on the table and said: "Here, wife, broil me a couple of these for breakfast. Ah! what's this I smell?

Fee-fi-fo-fum,
I smell the blood of an Englishman,
Be he alive, or be he dead
I'll grind his bones to make my bread."

"Nonsense, dear," said his wife, "you're dreaming. Or perhaps you smell the scraps of that little boy you liked so much for yesterday's dinner. Here, you go and have a wash and tidy up, and by the time you come back your breakfast will be ready for you."

So off the ogre went, and Jack was just going to jump out of the oven and run away when the woman told him not. "Wait till he's asleep," says she. "He always has a doze after breakfast."

Well, the ogre had his breakfast, and after that he goes to a big chest and takes out a couple of bags of gold, and down he sits and counts till at last his head began to nod and he began to snore till the whole house shook again.

Then Jack crept out on tiptoe from his oven, and as he was passing the ogre he took one of the bags of gold under his arm, and off he pelters till he came to the beanstalk, and then he threw down the bag of gold, which of course fell into his mother's garden, and then he climbed down and climbed down till at last he got home and told his mother and showed her the gold and said: "Well, mother, wasn't I right about the beans? They are really magical, you see."

So they lived on the bag of gold for some time, but at last they came to the end of it, and Jack made up his mind to try his luck once more up at the top of the beanstalk. So one fine morning he rose up early and got onto the beanstalk, and he climbed and he climbed and he climbed and he climbed and he climbed and he climbed till at last he came out onto the road again and up to the great big tall house he had been to before. There, sure enough, was the great big tall woman standing on the doorstep.

"Good morning, mum," says Jack, as bold as brass. "Could you be so good as to give me something to eat?"

"Go away, my boy," said the big tall woman, "or else my man will eat you up for breakfast. But aren't you the youngster who came here once before? Do you know, that very day, my man missed one of his bags of gold."

"That's strange, mum," says Jack. "I daresay I could tell you something about that, but I'm so hungry I can't speak till I've had something to eat."

Well the big tall woman was so curious that she took him in and gave him something to eat. But he had scarcely begun munching it as slowly as he could when thump! thump! thump! they heard the giant's footstep, and his wife hid Jack away in the oven.

All happened as it did before. In came the ogre as he did before, said "Fee-fi-fo-fum," and had his breakfast of three broiled oxen. Then he said: "Wife, bring me the hen that lays the golden eggs." So she brought it, and the ogre said "Lay," and it laid an egg all of gold. And then the ogre began to nod his head and to snore till the house shook.

Then Jack crept out of the oven on tiptoe and caught hold of the golden hen, and was off before you could say "Jack Robinson." But this time the hen gave a cackle which woke the ogre, and just as Jack got out of the house he heard him calling: "Wife, wife, what have you done with my golden hen?"

And the wife said: "Why, my dear?"

But that was all Jack heard, for he rushed off to the beanstalk and climbed down like a house on fire. And when he got home he showed his mother the wonderful hen and said "Lay," to it; and it laid a golden egg every time he said "Lay."

Well, Jack was not content, and it wasn't very long before he determined to have another try at his luck up there at the top of the beanstalk. So one fine morning he rose up early, and got onto the beanstalk, and he climbed and he climbed and he climbed and he climbed till he got to the top. But this time he knew better than to go straight to the ogre's house. And when he got near

This selection is from Thucydides' History of the Peloponnesian War, *which describes the conflict between Athens and Sparta that took place between 431 and 404 B.C. and involved most of the Greek city-states on one side or the other. Melos, a small island off the southeastern coast of Greece, tried to remain independent and neutral, resisting an Athenian attempt to make it a tributary. Athens then sent a second expedition to subjugate the island, or at least to force it into an alliance. Before giving the order to attack, the Athenian generals sent representatives to negotiate with the Melians. The meeting dealt with the issue of whether a great power should be swayed by anything except self-interest in dealing with a smaller power.*

THE MELIAN DIALOGUE

Thucydides

The next summer the Athenians made an expedition against the isle of Melos. The Melians are a colony of Lacedaemon that would not submit to the Athenians like the other islanders and at first remained neutral and took no part in the struggle, but afterwards, upon the Athenians using violence and plundering their territory, assumed an attitude of open hostility. The Athenian generals encamped in their territory with their army, and before doing any harm to their land sent envoys to negotiate. These the Melians did not bring before the people, but told them to state the object of their mission to the magistrates and the council. The Athenian envoys then said:

ATHENIANS: As we are not to speak to the people, for fear that if we made a single speech without interruption we might deceive them with attractive arguments to which there was no chance of replying— we realize that this is the meaning of our being brought before your ruling body— we suggest that you who sit here should make security doubly sure. Let us have no long speeches from you either, but deal separately with each point, and take up at once any statement of which you disapprove, and criticize it.

MELIANS: We have no objection to your reasonable suggestion that we should put our respective points of view quietly to each other, but the military preparations which you have already made seem inconsistent with it. We see that you have come to be yourselves the judges of the debate, and that its natural conclusion for us will be slavery if you convince us, and war if we get the better of the argument and therefore refuse to submit.

ATHENIANS: If you have met us in order to make surmises about the future, or for any other purpose than to look existing facts in the face and to discuss the safety of your city on this basis, we will break off the conversations; otherwise, we are ready to speak.

MELIANS: In our position it is natural and excusable to explore many ideas and arguments. But the problem that has brought us here is our security, so, if you think fit, let the discussion follow the line you propose.

ATHENIANS: Then we will not make a long and unconvincing speech, full of fine phrases, to prove that our victory over Persia justifies our empire, or that we are now attacking you because you have wronged us, and we ask you not to expect to convince us by saying that you have not injured us, or that, though a colony of Lacedaemon, you did not join her. Let each of us say what we really think and reach a practical agreement. You know and we know, as practical men, that the question of justice arises only between parties equal in strength, and that the strong do what they can and the weak submit.

MELIANS: As you ignore justice and have made self-interest the basis of discussion, we must take the same ground, and we say that in our opinion it is in your interest to maintain a principle which is for the good of all—that anyone in danger should have just and equitable treatment and any advantage, even if not strictly his due, which he can secure by persuasion. This is your interest as much as ours, for your fall would involve you in a crushing punishment that would be a lesson to the world.

ATHENIANS: We have no apprehensions about the fate of our empire, if it did fall; those who rule other peoples, like the Lacedaemonians, are not formidable to a defeated enemy. Nor is it the Lacedaemonians with whom we are now contending: the danger is from subjects who of themselves may attack and conquer their rulers. But leave that danger to us to face. At the moment we shall prove that we have come in the interest of our empire and that in what we shall say we are seeking the safety of your state; for we wish you to become our subjects with least trouble to ourselves, and we would like you to survive in our interests as well as your own.

MELIANS: It may be your interest to be our masters; how can it be ours to be your slaves?

ATHENIANS: By submitting you would avoid a terrible fate, and we should gain by not destroying you.

MELIANS: Would you not agree to an arrangement under which we should keep out of the war, and be your friends instead of your enemies, but neutral?

ATHENIANS: No; your hostility injures us less than your friendship. That, to our subjects, is an illustration of our weakness, while your hatred exhibits our power.

MELIANS: Is this the construction which your subjects put on it? Do they not distinguish between states in which you have no concern, and peoples who are most of them your colonies, and some conquered rebels?

ATHENIANS: They think that one nation has as good rights as another, but that some survive because they are strong and we are afraid to attack them. So, apart from the addition to our empire, your subjection would give us security: the fact that you are islanders (and weaker than others) makes it the more important that you should not get the better of the mistress of the sea.

MELIANS: But do you see no safety in our neutrality? You debar us from the plea of justice and press us to submit to your interests, so we must expound our own, and try to convince you, if the two happen to coincide. Will you not make enemies of all neutral Powers when they see your conduct and reflect that some day you will attack them? Will not your action strengthen your existing opponents, and induce those who would otherwise never be your enemies to become so against their will?

ATHENIANS: No. The mainland states, secure in their freedom, will be slow to take defensive measures against us, and we do not consider them so formidable as independent island powers like yourselves, or subjects already smarting under our yoke. These are most likely to take a thoughtless step and bring themselves and us into obvious danger.

MELIANS: Surely then, if you are ready to risk so much to maintain your empire, and the enslaved peoples so much to escape from it, it would be criminal cowardice in us, who are still free, not to take any and every measure before submitting to slavery?

ATHENIANS: No, if you reflect calmly: for this is not a competition in heroism between equals, where your honor is at stake, but a question of self-preservation, to save you from a struggle with a far stronger Power.

MELIANS: Still, we know that in war fortune is more impartial than the disproportion in numbers might lead one to expect. If we submit at once, our position is desperate; if we fight, there is still a hope that we shall stand secure.

ATHENIANS: Hope encourages men to take risks; men in a strong position may follow her without ruin, if not without loss. But when they stake all that they have to the last coin (for she is a spendthrift),

she reveals her real self in the hour of failure, and when her nature is known she leaves them without means of self-protection. You are weak, your future hangs on a turn of the scales; avoid the mistake most men make, who might save themselves by human means, and then, when visible hopes desert them, in their extremity turn to the invisible—prophecies and oracles and all those things which delude men with hopes, to their destruction.

MELIANS: We too, you can be sure, realize the difficulty of struggling against your power and against Fortune if she is not impartial. Still we trust that Heaven will not allow us to be worsted by Fortune, for in this quarrel we are right and you are wrong. Besides, we expect the support of Lacedaemon to supply the deficiencies in our strength, for she is bound to help us as her kinsmen, if for no other reason, and from a sense of honor. So our confidence is not entirely unreasonable.

ATHENIANS: As for divine favor, we think that we can count on it as much as you, for neither our claims nor our actions are inconsistent with what men believe about Heaven or desire for themselves. We believe that Heaven, and we know that men, by a natural law, always rule where they are stronger. We did not make that law nor were we the first to act on it; we found it existing, and it will exist forever, after we are gone; and we know that you and anyone else as strong as we are would do as we do. As to your expectations from Lacedaemon and your belief that she will help you from a sense of honor, we congratulate you on your innocence but we do not admire your folly. So far as they themselves and their national traditions are concerned, the Lacedaemonians are a highly virtuous people; as for their behavior to others, much might be said, but we can put it shortly by saying that, most obviously of all people we know, they identify their interests with justice and the pleasantest course with honor. Such principles do not favor your present irrational hopes of deliverance.

MELIANS: That is the chief reason why we have confidence in them now; in their own interest they will not wish to betray their own colonists and so help their enemies and destroy the confidence that their friends in Greece feel in them.

ATHENIANS: Apparently you do not realize that safety and self-interest go together, while the path of justice and honor is dangerous; and danger is a risk which the Lacedaemonians are little inclined to run.

MELIANS: Our view is that they would be more likely to run a risk in our case, and would regard it as less hazardous, because our nearness to Peloponnese makes it easier for them to act and our kinship gives them more confidence in us than in others.

ATHENIANS: Yes, but an intending ally looks not to the goodwill of those who invoke his aid but to marked superiority of real power, and of none is this truer than of the Lacedaemonians. They mistrust their own resources and attack their neighbors only when they have numerous allies, so it is not likely that, while we are masters of the sea, they would cross it to an island.

MELIANS: They might send others. The sea of Crete is large, and this will make it more difficult for its masters to capture hostile ships than for these to elude them

safely. If they failed by sea, they would attack your country and those of your allies whom Brasidas* did not reach; and then you will have to fight not against a country in which you have no concern, but for your own country and your allies' lands.

ATHENIANS: Here experience may teach you like others, and you will learn that Athens has never abandoned a siege from fear of another foe. You said that you proposed to discuss the safety of your city, but we observe that in all your speeches you have never said a word on which any reasonable expectation of it could be founded. Your strength lies in deferred hopes; in comparison with the forces now arrayed against you, your resources are too small for any hope of success. You will show a great want of judgment if you do not come to a more reasonable decision after we have withdrawn. Surely you will not fall back on the idea of honor, which has been the ruin of so many when danger and disgrace were staring them in the face. How often, when men have seen the fate to which they were tending, have they been enslaved by a phrase and drawn by the power of this seductive word to fall of their own free will into irreparable disaster, bringing on themselves by their folly a greater dishonor than fortune could inflict! If you are wise, you will avoid that fate. The greatest of cities makes you a fair offer, to keep your own land and become her tributary ally: there is no dishonor in that. The choice between war and safety is given you; do not obstinately take the worse alternative. The most successful people are those who stand

---

* *Brasidas.* A courageous and aggressive Spartan general who won many victories against the Athenians and their allies before he was killed in the tenth year of the war.

up to their equals, behave properly to their superiors, and treat their inferiors fairly. Think it over when we withdraw, and reflect once and again that you have only one country, and that its prosperity or ruin depends on one decision.

The Athenians now withdrew from the conference; and the Melians, left to themselves, came to a decision corresponding with what they had maintained in the discussion, and answered, "Our resolution, Athenians, is unaltered. We will not in a moment deprive of freedom a city that has existed for seven hundred years; we put our trust in the fortune by which the gods have preserved it until now, and in the help of men, that is, of the Lacedaemonians; and so we will try and save ourselves. Meanwhile we invite you to allow us to be friends to you and foes to neither party, and to retire from our country after making such a treaty as shall seem fit to us both."

Such was the answer of the Melians. The Athenians broke up the conference saying, "To judge from your decision, you are unique in regarding the future as more certain than the present and in allowing your wishes to convert the unseen into reality; and as you have staked most on, and trusted most in, the Lacedaemonians, your fortune, and your hopes, so will you be most completely deceived."

The Athenian envoys now returned to the army; and as the Melians showed no signs of yielding, the generals at once began hostilities, and drew a line of circumvallation round the Melians, dividing the work among the different states. Subsequently the Athenians returned with most of their army, leaving behind them a certain number of their own citizens and of the allies to keep guard by land and sea. The force thus left stayed on and besieged the place.

Meanwhile the Athenians at Pylos took so much plunder from the Lacedaemonians that the latter, although they still refrained from breaking off the treaty and going to war with Athens, proclaimed that any of their people that chose might plunder the Athenians. The Corinthians also commenced hostilities with the Athenians for private quarrels of their own; but the rest of the Peloponnesians stayed quiet. Meanwhile the Melians in a night attack took the part of the Athenian lines opposite the market, killed some of its garrison, and brought in corn and as many useful stores as they could. Then, retiring, they remained inactive, while the Athenians took measures to keep better guard in future.

Summer was now over. The next winter the Lacedaemonians intended to invade the Argive territory, but on arriving at the frontier found the sacrifices for crossing unfavorable, and went back again. This intention of theirs made the Argives suspicious of certain of their fellow citizens, some of whom they arrested; others, however, escaped them. About the same time the Melians again took another part of the Athenian lines which were but feebly garrisoned. In consequence reinforcements were sent from Athens, and the siege was now pressed vigorously; there was some treachery in the town, and the Melians surrendered at discretion to the Athenians, who put to death all the grown men whom they took, and sold the women and children for slaves; subsequently they sent out five hundred settlers and colonized the island.

Building Your Answer in Shared Inquiry Discussion

Name: _____

Story Title: _____

Your leader's question: _____

_____

_____

Your answer before discussion: _____

_____

_____

_____

After discussion, did you . . . (circle one)

| Change your mind? How? | Keep the same answer? Why? | Hear a new idea that you liked? What? |

_____

_____

_____

_____

Distinguishing Factual, Interpretive, and Evaluative Questions

EXERCISE FOR "JACK AND THE BEANSTALK"

For each of the following questions, indicate with an "F," "I," or "E" whether the question is factual, interpretive, or evaluative.

_____   1. Why does Jack show his mother every item he steals from the ogre?

_____   2. Why does the ogre become suspicious that a stranger is present?

_____   3. Why does stealing often make people greedy for more?

_____   4. Is the author sarcastic when he calls Jack's reply to the old man "sharp as a needle"?

_____   5. Does Jack plan to steal from the ogre when he climbs the beanstalk for the first time?

_____   6. Do you agree with the story that Jack was right to take advantage of his opportunities?

_____   7. Why does the ogre's wife want to keep Jack from being eaten on his first trip up the beanstalk?

Asking Follow-up Questions

EXERCISE FOR "A GAME OF CATCH"

Each of the following sequences consists of a leader's question and a participant's response. For each sequence, write the follow-up question you would ask, taking into account both the participant's response and the leader's question.

1. **Leader:** According to the story, do Glennie and Monk treat Scho unfairly?

   Participant: No, on the whole they behave very well toward a pushy kid.

   Your Follow-up Question:

2. **Leader:** Why do Monk and Glennie ignore what Scho says after he finds a seat in the tree?

   Participant: What did Scho say?

   Your Follow-up Question:

3. **Leader:** Why does Monk begin to throw the ball to Glennie once or twice before he gives Scho his grounder?

   Participant: Because Scho failed to catch one of the balls that Monk threw him.

   Your Follow-up Question:

4. **Leader:** Just before Scho falls, why is his voice both "exuberant and panicky"?

   Participant: I don't think I could have those two feelings at the same time.

   Your Follow-up Question:

5. **Leader:** Why does Scho enlarge the scope of his game at the end of the story?

   Participant: I don't know.

   Your Follow-up Question:

6. **Leader:** Why does Scho tease the boys mainly while he is in the tree?

   Participant 1: Playing his game from the tree gives Scho a false sense of power because he is looking down on Glennie and Monk.

   Participant 2: Scho feels safe from any attempt of Glennie and Monk's to shut him up.

   Your Follow-up Question:

APPENDIX B:

SAMPLE CURRICULUM UNITS

"The King of the Frogs"

"Secret Messages" Poetry Unit

"Jack and the Beanstalk"

"A Game of Catch"

"The Melian Dialogue"

THE KING OF THE FROGS

AFRICAN FOLKTALE

AS TOLD BY

HUMPHREY HARMAN

O V E R V I E W

SESSION 1

This session consists of an introduction and first reading of the story, followed by a brief sharing of questions and comments, a performance of the frogs' chorus, and an art activity in which children draw their interpretation of the frogs.

AT-HOME WORK

During this second reading, the adult partner encourages the child to join in saying the underlined words and phrases, and pauses to discuss G.B.'s three questions. Children respond to these questions by circling their answers.

After reading, the adult writes the child's own question about the story into the book in preparation for the Sharing Questions Discussion (Session 4).

SESSION 2

During this reading of the story, you will collect students' responses to G.B.'s questions and lead a discussion of them. The session concludes with an art activity in which children draw their interpretation of Mmumi.

SESSION 3

This session consists of an evaluative discussion in which children consider other ways the frogs could have made their lives orderly, and an art activity in which children draw their interpretation of King Mamba and the frogs.

SESSION 4

This session consists of a Sharing Questions Discussion and a group creative-writing activity in which students compose a poem about quiet fun and noisy fun.

SESSION 1

INTRODUCTION

Begin the session by telling your class that this is a story from Africa. Write on the board the names "Mmumi," "Gogo," and "Mamba," and ask children to repeat them after you.

FIRST READING AND SHARING OF RESPONSES

Ask children to listen as you read the story aloud. After the reading, allow a few moments to clear up unfamiliar vocabulary and to let students ask questions and share their initial reactions to the story. Encourage children to offer their opinions about which parts of the story they especially liked and why.

CHORAL ACTIVITY

Reread the first paragraph of the story, which describes the different kinds of noises the frogs make. After you read the description of each noise, have children practice making it. When the paragraph is finished, divide the children into five groups, one for each noise. Let children combine their noises into a "Frog Chorus." Then have them practice becoming suddenly so quiet "you can hear the whole world breathe."

ART ACTIVITY

Have children turn to the frontispiece, captioned "The Frogs Do As They Please." Tell them that they are going to draw a picture of what they think the frogs' life is like at the beginning of the story, when the frogs do as they please. Help children get ideas for their pictures by asking such questions as *Do you think the noise and untidiness would have been fun or unpleasant? Why do the frogs all want to shout at once?*

Allow time for students to share and compare their drawings.

SESSION 2

POSTING "MY QUESTIONS"

Have students cut out the questions they wrote at home and pin them on the Sharing Questions bulletin board. Children who have not had an at-home reading can dictate their questions to you at this time. Encourage children to look at the Sharing Questions bulletin board during the week, to point out their own questions and to ask about those of their classmates.

READING AND REVIEW OF G.B.'S QUESTIONS

Read the story aloud, encouraging students to follow along in their books. Pause to collect students' responses to G.B.'s questions (pages 12, 14, and 16). To help students think further about their responses, ask additional questions such as those given in the margin of your text.

SESSION 2 (continued)

ART ACTIVITY

Ask students to turn to the page captioned "Mmumi." Tell them that they are going to draw a picture of Mmumi, showing what kind of personality they think he has. If you think it necessary, review some of the ideas about Mmumi that children brought up earlier in the session when discussing G.B.'s questions.

Allow time for students to share and compare their drawings.

SESSION 3

EVALUATIVE DISCUSSION

Introduce the activity by reminding children that at the beginning of the story the frogs do as they please and do not like it, while at the end they have a king who keeps them orderly but also eats frogs. Tell students that now they will have a chance to think about other ways in which the frogs might have been able to lead an orderly life.

Briefly outline three possibilities: choosing one of the frogs to be king, having as king a more powerful animal who doesn't eat frogs, or making rules for themselves without the help of a king. Write on the board the headings "Frog King," "Other Animal King," and "Make Their Own Rules." Ask children which situation they think would have been best for the frogs and have them give their reasons, with support from the story. Write down children's ideas under the appropriate heading.

After the class has debated the question for five or ten minutes, ask children to turn to the page at the end of the story with the heading "What do *you* think the frogs should do?" Have children circle their answer and write their reason on the lines provided.

ART ACTIVITY

Have children turn to the page at the end of the story captioned "King Mamba and His Subjects." Read aloud the last two paragraphs of the story, beginning "The frogs developed the greatest respect...." Help students think about different ways the frogs might feel about having Mamba as king by asking such questions as *Is the frogs' life terrible or not so bad with Mamba as king? Do they like being orderly after all? Do the frogs dislike Mamba? Are they proud to have such a fierce king?*

Then have students draw pictures of Mamba and the frogs. Allow time for students to share and compare their drawings.

SESSION 4

SHARING QUESTIONS DISCUSSION

Prepare for discussion as usual, deciding on the five or six interpretive questions you intend to ask the class. Note which of the children's questions are similar to those you plan to lead and try to include three or four of their questions in your final list. When you write your questions on the board, include children's names as appropriate.

Suggested Interpretive Questions

Why does the wise old frog go back to Mmumi after Gogo doesn't work out?

Are the frogs better off with Mamba to keep them orderly than they were when they lived in disorder at the beginning of the story?

Why do the frogs need a king to keep them orderly?

GROUP CREATIVE WRITING

Remind students that at the end of the story the frogs live quietly, something they could not do before, though sometimes they "break out" in noise as they used to do. Tell children that now they are going to create a poem about quiet fun and noisy fun. Ask the class to think briefly about things they enjoy doing that are quiet, and things they enjoy doing that are noisy.

Then write on the board, "In a quiet mood, I…" and ask the class to suggest lines describing quiet fun. Encourage students to make their lines descriptive, showing how the quietness is important to the fun. Write their lines on the board. When you have collected several lines, write "In a noisy mood, I…" and repeat the process for noisy fun.

When the poem is completed, prepare copies for children to paste into their books, or ask them to copy the entire poem or their favorite lines on the page titled "Quiet and Noisy."

The Frogs Do As They Please

Have you ever been beside a lake in Africa at night and listened to the frogs? You haven't? Then you cannot imagine what the noise is like. And it's not just one kind of noise, it's several. Over there for instance are a thousand creaking doors that have never had their hinges oiled and someone opens and shuts them—and keeps on doing just that. Over *there* are a thousand fat men snoring and no one wakes them up. Then there are a thousand carpenters sawing planks and all the saws want a touch of grease, and a thousand little bells are being struck and a thousand corks are being pulled out of bottles.

Noise! You can hardly hear yourself think.

Then you go a little closer until you
can just see the edge of the water
and perhaps a reed or two and there
is silence. Just the splash of a frog jumping
into the water late because he was asleep
and didn't hear you coming. Then
nothing, and you can hear the whole
world breathe.

There's a story about this.

Long ago the frogs did as they pleased and the result was dreadful. Not one of them would listen to what another said and they all shouted at once. Children wouldn't obey their parents and even wives wouldn't listen to their husbands, which is, indeed, something hardly to be understood. It was all noisy and untidy beyond bearing and nothing ever got done.

At last a wise, wise old frog called everyone to a meeting and, since he had a very fine voice and went on shouting for long enough, he managed to get them all there at once, for to tell you the truth they were pretty sick of living the way they did.

"Frogs!" said the old frog, puffing himself up. "We cannot go on like this. It's no sort of life for anyone and, anyway, when you see how all the other creatures live it makes one ashamed of being a frog. There is only one thing to do. We must get a king. When people have kings there is peace and order and everyone does as he is told."

"Agreed!" they all shouted and they stayed long enough to commission the old frog to see what he could do about getting them one, before everybody fell to quarreling and pushing and splashing and the meeting broke up in disorder. As usual.

Then the wise, wise old frog went to see the Great God **Mmumi** (you will say the two *m*'s correctly if you hum a little before you begin the word). Mmumi happened to be in charge of that part of the world.

Mmumi

He is a very slow god and usually gives people more than they bargain for. He agreed drowsily that the frogs needed a king and promised to do something about it. Then he went to sleep again.

So the frogs went on as usual, which was badly, until one day Mmumi woke up, remembered his promise, took a great green mossy boulder which had the rough shape of a gigantic frog and threw it into the water. **SPLASH!**

"There you are!" he shouted (it sounded like thunder). "There's your king. His name's Gogo and like me he doesn't want to be disturbed. Respect him and be satisfied."

Do you think Mmumi gives the frogs Gogo because Mmumi is:

LAZY

WISE

MAKING FUN OF THEM

(Circle your answer.)

The whole lake was shaken by Gogo's fall. The waves washed through the reeds and tore up the shore, and in the middle of a great cloud of mud Gogo settled on the bottom and the fat green waterweeds curled round and over him. He looked shocking.

The frogs were terrified and fled under stones and into dark corners and holes under the bank. Their long white legs streaked behind them as they swam. Parents found their children and husbands their wives and then settled down to explaining what had happened.

"This is our king," they said, "and a fine terrible one he seems, and from the splash he made not the sort to fool about with. Now all will be well and this scandalous behavior will stop."

And so it did, for a while.

But although Gogo had made such a wonderful first impression, as time passed they noticed that he never moved. He just sat quietly in the mud and stared in the same direction. Presently they began to get used to him, until finally some young, bold, bad frogs ventured to swim close to him and then one of them touched his nose.

And still Gogo said and did nothing.

"**Bah! He's not a king!**" they shouted. "**He's not even a frog.** He's just an old stone and couldn't hurt anyone." And they swam round him until they were dizzy and jumped all over his back and went away and spoke rudely about him to their elders.

Do you agree that the young frogs are "bad"? (Circle your answer.)

YES   NO

Why or why not?

At first none of the elders believed them. They had told their children Gogo was a king and a king he had to be, but soon it was impossible to deny that the children were right and then.... Well, the noise began again and things were as they had always been, only worse. **Terrible!**

The wise, wise old frog sighed and set out to see Mmumi again, who was not at all pleased at being woken a second time.

"All right!" he shouted in a passion. "*All right!* You aren't satisfied with the king I've given you. Is that the way it is? Very well, you shall have another and I hope you like him."

And the very next night he gave them Mamba the Crocodile.

Gogo had come to his people with a splash that shook the lake

but Mamba slid into the water with only
a whisper and left but one small
ring spreading gently to show that he
had come. Then he swam, silent
as a shadow, lithe and long and secret,
his jaws grinning like a trap. Gogo
had never visited the people he had been
given to rule but Mamba visited them
often and suddenly, and whenever he met
a subject the great jaws gaped and closed
and often it was the last of that frog.

The frogs developed the greatest
respect for their new king and lived
quietly, looking over the backs of their
heads as frogs can. Now and again at
night they break out but they keep their
ears open and if you go near the lake
they shut up.

They think that it's Mamba coming to
put a little order into them and they
keep quiet.

Does Mmumi give
the frogs Mamba for
a king to punish
them or to make
their life better?
(Circle your answer.)

TO PUNISH THEM

TO MAKE THEIR
LIFE BETTER

King Mamba and His Subjects

What do *you* think the frogs should do? (Circle one.)

1. Have a frog king

2. Have another animal as king

3. Make their own rules

Why? _____

_____

_____

_____

Quiet and Noisy

In a quiet mood, I _____

_____

_____

_____

_____

In a noisy mood, I _____

_____

_____

_____

_____

My Question

Name

SECRET MESSAGES

POETRY BY

ROBERT LOUIS STEVENSON,

BARBARA JUSTER ESBENSEN,

AND

EMILY DICKINSON

SESSION 1: "The Dumb Soldier"

This session consists of an introduction, two readings of the poem, and an art activity in which children draw their interpretation of the "fairy things" the soldier sees in the grass.

AT-HOME WORK: "The Dumb Soldier"

The adult partner reads the poem through once, encouraging the child to join in saying the underlined phrases. The adult then reads the poem a second time, pausing to discuss G.B.'s two questions.

After reading, the adult writes the child's own question about "The Dumb Soldier" into the book in preparation for the Sharing Questions Discussion (Session 2).

SESSION 2: "The Dumb Soldier"

During this reading of the poem, you will collect students' responses to G.B.'s questions and lead a brief discussion of them. The session concludes with a Sharing Questions Discussion and an art activity in which students draw a world they would like to experience.

SESSION 3: "Snow Print Two: Hieroglyphics"

This session consists of an introduction and first reading of the poem, a second reading and discussion of the poem, and a group writing and art activity in which children compose their own bird secrets in picture writing.

SESSION 4: "Bee! I'm Expecting You!"

This session consists of an introduction and first reading of the poem, a second reading and discussion of the poem, and a group writing and art activity in which children compose the bee's reply to the fly and draw a picture of the bee and the fly together.

SESSION 1: "The Dumb Soldier"

INTRODUCTION

Introduce the poem by explaining to children that it is about a boy who plays with his toy soldier. The soldier is called "dumb" because it cannot speak, and it is made of *lead*, a heavy kind of metal. A *grenadier* is a special kind of soldier.

FIRST AND SECOND READINGS

Ask children to listen as you read the poem aloud. Before reading the poem a second time, take a few moments to let children ask questions and make comments. Also help children clear up such unfamiliar vocabulary as "apace," "scythe is stoned," and "disclose," using the definitions given in the margin of your text.

Then encourage children to follow along in their books as you read the poem aloud a second time. Ask them to join in chorusing the fifth stanza—the turning point of the poem—and the last stanza.

ART ACTIVITY

Have students turn to the page captioned "What the Soldier Sees" and tell them that they will have a chance to imagine what kinds of "fairy things" the toy soldier sees in the "forests of the grass." Help them get ideas for their drawings by asking such questions as *What games might you play among tall grass and spring flowers? If you were so tiny that grass seemed like trees, what creatures might you meet? What kind of magic would you find?* Allow time for children to share and compare their illustrations.

SESSION 2: "The Dumb Soldier"

POSTING "MY QUESTIONS"

Have students cut out the questions they wrote at home. Glance through them briefly and note any you would like to include in the Sharing Questions Discussion before pinning them on the Sharing Questions bulletin board.

READING AND REVIEW OF G.B.'S QUESTIONS

Read the poem aloud, pausing after the fifth stanza and the last stanza to collect responses to G.B.'s questions. Encourage students to give reasons for their answers and then help them think further about the poem by asking additional questions such as those printed in the margin of your text.

SHARING QUESTIONS DISCUSSION

Move directly from your review of G.B.'s second question into the Sharing Questions Discussion. When you write your questions on the board, note which of your questions are similar to the children's and include their names as appropriate.

Suggested Interpretive Questions

Why does the boy think his soldier can see "fairy things" in the grass?

Why does the boy choose a soldier instead of another toy?

Why does the boy imagine that the soldier can see but not speak?

Why does the boy want to make up the soldier's tale himself?

SESSION 2: "The Dumb Soldier" (continued)

ART ACTIVITY

Remind children that the boy in the poem says he would like to live in the grass, like his toy soldier. Ask students to think about places in the world they would like to see but can't because they are people. Would they like to live in the ocean and play with seals and whales? Or fly among the birds? What would they see, hear, and learn there?

Have students turn to the page captioned "I would like to see..." and ask them to draw that place. As children work, circulate among them and help them complete their captions. Allow time for students to share and compare their drawings.

SESSION 3: "Snow Print Two: Hieroglyphics"

INTRODUCTION

Tell students that "hieroglyphics" is a special kind of writing that uses pictures instead of letters. In this poem, the hieroglyphics are the marks the birds make on the snow with their feet.

FIRST READING

Read the poem through while children listen. Before reading the poem a second time, take a few moments to let children ask questions and make comments, and clear up unfamiliar vocabulary.

SECOND READING AND DISCUSSION

As you read the poem a second time, encourage students to follow along in their books. When you have finished, help students think further about the communication between the birds and the person speaking in the poem by asking such questions as *Why is the person in the poem able to "read" the birds' secret messages? Why does the person think the messages are for him or her? How do you think the speaker feels about the birds' messages? Why do the birds' footprints make the speaker think of lost songs and cold wind?*

GROUP CREATIVE WRITING AND ART ACTIVITY

Ask students to think of other "scribbled secrets" the birds might have. Label a section of the board "Bird Secrets" and collect several examples from the class.

Tell children that they are going to write their own bird secrets in picture writing. As an example to help them get started, write on another section of the board "the howling wind that claws like a cat." Have the class briefly suggest some ways this phrase could be written in pictures. (You might ask a few volunteers to draw examples on the board.)

Then ask students to turn to the page titled "Messages From a Bird." Have them look back over the list of "Bird Secrets" on the board and write the ones they like best in their own picture writing.

Allow time for children to share their messages and to try reading each other's picture writing. They can also write the English "translations" under each line of picture writing.

SESSION 4: "Bee! I'm Expecting You!"

INTRODUCTION

Introduce the session by telling students that the poem they are going to hear is a letter written to a bee by a friend. (Let children be surprised to discover at the end of the poem that the friend is a fly.)

FIRST READING

Ask children to listen as you read the poem aloud. Before reading the poem a second time, take a few moments to let children ask questions and make comments, and clear up unfamiliar vocabulary.

SECOND READING AND DISCUSSION

Read the poem a second time, encouraging students to follow along in their books and to join in saying the phrases "Bee! I'm expecting you!" and "Or better, be with me—/Yours, Fly."

After the reading, briefly review with students things that bees and flies have in common. Then help students think about the friendship between the fly and the bee in this poem by asking such questions as *The fly says he was talking yesterday to somebody the bee knows—who could that be? Why does the fly say the frogs are at work? What is the frogs' job? Why is the fly so eager for the bee to come back?*

GROUP CREATIVE WRITING AND ART ACTIVITY

Tell students that they are going to write the bee's reply to the fly's letter by thinking about some of the things the bee would look forward to doing with the fly when she returns. Write students' suggestions on the board as they offer them. You may want to help students get ideas by asking such questions as *When the bee and the fly get together, will they mostly work or play? Will the bee and the fly do anything special, or just be together? Will they do things by themselves, or with other creatures?*

Then have students turn to the page with the heading "Dear Fly." Ask them to write their own letters from the bee or to copy their favorite lines from the board.

After students have finished writing, they can illustrate the page by drawing what they think the fly and the bee will do when they get together. Allow time for children to share and compare their drawings.

What the Soldier Sees

THE DUMB SOLDIER

When the grass was closely mown,
Walking on the lawn alone,
In the turf a hole I found
And hid a soldier underground.

Spring and daisies came apace;
Grasses hide my hiding-place;
Grasses run like a green sea
O'er the lawn up to my knee.

Under grass alone he lies,
Looking up with leaden eyes,
Scarlet coat and pointed gun,
To the stars and to the sun.

When the grass is ripe like grain,
When the scythe is stoned again,
When the lawn is shaven clear,
Then my hole shall reappear.

I shall find him, never fear,
I shall find my grenadier;
But for all that's gone and come,
I shall find my soldier dumb.

Why do you think
the boy hides his
soldier in the
ground?

He has lived, a little thing,
In the grassy woods of spring;
Done, if he could tell me true,
Just as I should like to do.

He has seen the starry hours
And the springing of the flowers;
And the fairy things that pass
In the forests of the grass.

In the silence he has heard
Talking bee and ladybird,
And the butterfly has flown
O'er him as he lay alone.

<u>Not a word will he disclose,</u>
<u>Not a word of all he knows.</u>
<u>I must lay him on the shelf,</u>
<u>And make up the tale myself.</u>

—Robert Louis Stevenson

Why would the boy like to live in the grass, like his soldier?

I would like to see _____

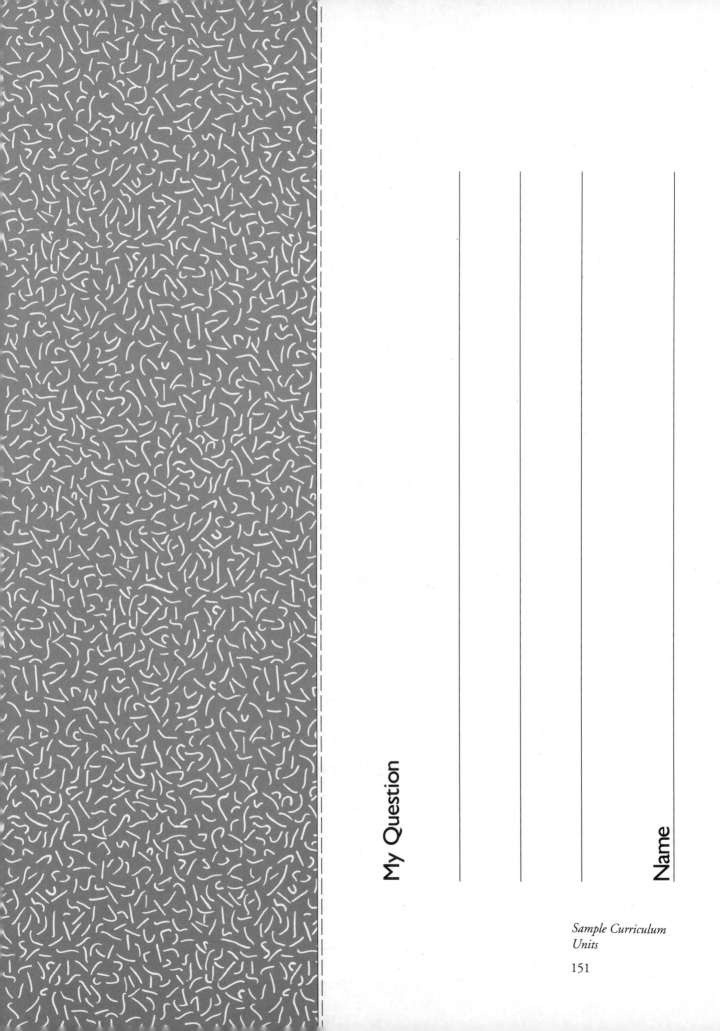

My Question

Name

SNOW PRINT TWO: HIEROGLYPHICS

In the alley
under the last cold rung
of the fire escape
birds are printing
the new snow
with a narrow alphabet.

Their scribbled secrets
tell of lost songs
and the howling wind
that claws like a cat.

These are messages
from the small dark birds
to me.

—Barbara Juster Esbensen

Messages From a Bird

1. _____

   _____

2. _____

   _____

3. _____

   _____

BEE! I'M EXPECTING YOU!

Bee! I'm expecting you!
Was saying Yesterday
To Somebody you know
That you were due—

The Frogs got Home last Week—
Are settled, and at work—
Birds, mostly back—
The Clover warm and thick—

You'll get my Letter by
The seventeenth; Reply
Or better, be with me—
Yours, Fly.

—Emily Dickinson

Dear Fly,

_____

_____

_____

_____

Yours,

Bee

Jack and the Beanstalk

*English folktale
as told by Joseph Jacobs*

SESSION 1

First reading of the story, followed by a sharing of initial questions and reactions.

Students write down a question they have about the story.

AT-HOME WORK

Second reading of the story, with discussion of the three at-home questions.

SESSION 2

Third reading of the story, pausing to discuss students' responses to the at-home questions.

Students write an explanation of why they think they are or are not like Jack.

SESSION 3

Textual analysis of the scene in which Jack trades his cow for the beans and takes the beans home to show his mother, followed by comparative dramatizations of this scene.

Students write an explanation of why they think Jack is or is not acting grown-up in this part of the story.

SESSION 4

Shared Inquiry Discussion: while half the class participates in discussion, the other half draws their interpretation of the ogre.

Optional Activity: students choose a question from the JGB bulletin board and write their answers.

SESSION 5

Creative Writing: students imagine an interview with the princess who marries Jack. (See Appendix A for the corresponding activity page master.)

Activities for Jack and the Beanstalk

Before reading the story, tell students that it is an English fairy tale about a boy named Jack, who climbs to the sky on a magic beanstalk and meets an ogre. Explain that an *ogre* is a hideous giant that eats people.

After the reading, have students share their initial questions and reactions to the story. Then ask them to write down a question, either one of their own or another one that they heard and liked. Post their questions on the JGB bulletin board. Encourage students to read them during the week and to select one they would like to answer after Shared Inquiry Discussion.

SESSION 2

Read the story aloud while students follow along in their books. Pause at the at-home questions to collect students' responses, and ask follow-up questions such as those given in the margin of your text.

Conclude the session by writing on the board:

> I think I (am/am not) like Jack because _____ .

Have your students think over their answers to the at-home questions. Then tell them to copy and complete the sentence on the board by writing in either "am" or "am not" and giving a reason for their choice.

SESSION 3

Begin the session by telling students that they are going to look closely at the part of the story in which Jack trades his cow for the beans and takes the beans home to show his mother.

Have students follow along as you read aloud the bracketed passage on pages 142-145. Conduct a textual analysis, asking questions such as those provided in the margin of your text.

Afterward, have students act out the scene. Select two casts by picking students who have different interpretations of the characters—for example, a smart Jack and a foolish Jack; a nice, helpful old man and a strange, mysterious old man; a mother who has good reason to scold Jack and a mother who gets much too angry.

When both performances are finished, invite the class to compare the different versions. If your students wish, you may want to let them perform additional interpretations of the scene.

Conclude the session by writing on the board:

> In this part of the story, I think Jack (is/is not) acting grown-up because _____ .

Tell students to copy and complete this sentence by writing in either "is" or "is not" and giving a reason for their choice.

SESSION 4

While you lead half the class in Shared Inquiry Discussion, have the rest of your students draw their interpretations of the ogre at any point in the story. Tell students that they can include other characters, such as Jack or the ogre's wife, in their pictures. Encourage them to write captions explaining their pictures.

Below are sample interpretive questions to help you prepare for discussion.

Why does Jack decide to climb the beanstalk the third time?

1. Why isn't Jack "content," even though he has a hen that lays golden eggs?

2. Why does Jack think he will be lucky for a third time?

3. Why isn't Jack afraid of being eaten by the ogre?

4. Why does Jack risk his life by taking the singing harp?

5. Does Jack return to the ogre's house because he enjoys outsmarting the ogre, or because he wants to punish him?

Why is the ogre's wife kinder to Jack than his own mother is?

1. Why doesn't Jack's mother believe him when he tells her the beans are magical?

2. Why doesn't Jack show his mother that the beans really were magical before he climbs the beanstalk?

3. Why does the ogre's wife want to keep Jack from being eaten on his first trip?

4. Why is the ogre's wife kind to Jack on his second visit, even though she suspects that he stole her husband's money?

5. Why does Jack know better than to ask the ogre's wife for help a third time?

Why does Jack grow up successfully in this story?

1. Why is Jack confident that he will be able to sell Milky-white, a cow that no longer gives milk?

2. Why does Jack listen to what the funny-looking old man tells him?

3. Why is Jack so proud of himself for deciding to trade Milky-white for five "magical" beans?

4. Why doesn't Jack run away when the ogre's wife warns him that her husband eats boys?

5. Why doesn't Jack hesitate to take the ogre's bag of gold, the hen that lays the golden eggs, and the singing harp?

6. Do things turn out well for Jack mainly because of luck and magic or mainly because of his own cleverness?

Optional Activity: ask students to write answers to their favorite question from the JGB bulletin board.

Activities for Jack and the Beanstalk

Introduce the activity by telling students that together they are going to imagine an interview with the great princess who marries Jack.

Distribute the Writing After Discussion activity page to the class. Tell students that the first interview question is provided for them, but that they will be thinking of a few more questions to ask the princess. Write students' additional questions on the board. If students need help coming up with questions, you can suggest some yourself, such as:

What do you think your life will be like after you marry Jack?

Do you think Jack has any faults?

What will you and Jack do for fun?

Then have students work in pairs or small groups to answer the question on the activity page and two more questions of their choice. They can copy questions from the board or come up with their own. Remind students to answer the interview questions as if *they* were the princess.

Allow time for students to share their interviews with the class.

Writing After Discussion　　　　　　JACK AND THE BEANSTALK

Name: _____

An Interview with the Princess

Question: What does a great princess like you admire about Jack?

Answer: _____

_____

_____

Question: _____

_____

Answer: _____

_____

_____

Question: _____

_____

Answer: _____

_____

_____

Junior Great Books Series 2. © 1992 by The Great Books Foundation.

Why does the old man ask Jack such an odd question before offering to swap the beans for Jack's cow?

Why does the man say he doesn't mind doing a swap because Jack is so sharp?

Does Jack believe what the man tells him about the beans?

Would **you** *trade Milky-white for the strange-looking beans? Why do you think Jack does?*

Why does Jack think he's getting a good bargain?

Why does Jack think it would be a good thing to have beans that grow right up to the sky overnight?

...

"We've tried that before, and nobody would take you," said his mother. "We must sell Milky-white and with the money start a shop or something."

"All right, mother," says Jack. "It's market day today, and I'll soon sell Milky-white, and then we'll see what we can do."

So he took the cow's halter in his hand, and off he started. He hadn't gone far when he met a funny-looking old man who said to him: "Good morning, Jack."

"Good morning to you," said Jack, and wondered how he knew his name.

"Well, Jack, and where are you off to?" said the man.

"I'm going to market to sell our cow here."

...

"Oh, you look the proper sort of <u>chap</u> to sell cows," said the man. "I wonder if you know how many beans make five."

"Two in each hand and one in your mouth," says Jack, as sharp as a needle.

"Right you are," says the man. "And here they are, the very beans themselves," he went on, pulling out of his pocket a number of strange-looking beans. "As you are so sharp," says he, "I don't mind doing a swap with you—your cow for these beans."

"Go along," says Jack. "Wouldn't you like it?"

"Ah! you don't know what these beans are," said the man. "If you plant them overnight, by morning they grow right up to the sky."

"Really?" says Jack. "You don't say so."

"Yes, that is so, and if it doesn't turn out to be true you can have your cow back."

"Right," says Jack, and hands him over Milky-white's halter and pockets the beans.

143

Would you trade Milky-white for the strange-looking beans? Why do you think Jack does?

chap: fellow

NOTE: Teacher's Editions contain the entire student text, with annotations; we show here only those pages on which students' at-home questions appear.

Sample Curriculum Units

and up and up till it reached the sky. So the man spoke truth after all.

The beanstalk grew up quite close past Jack's window, so all he had to do was to open it and give a jump onto the beanstalk, which ran up just like a big ladder. So Jack climbed, and he climbed and he climbed and he climbed and he climbed and he climbed and he climbed till at last he reached the sky. And when he got there he found a long broad road going as straight as a dart. So he walked along and he walked along and he walked along till he came to a great big tall house, and on the doorstep there was a great big tall woman.

Would you climb a beanstalk that reached to the sky? Why do you think Jack does?

"Good morning, mum," says Jack, quite polite-like. "Could you be so kind as to give me some breakfast?" For he hadn't had anything to eat, you know, the night before and was as hungry as a hunter.

"It's breakfast you want, is it?" says the great big tall woman. "It's breakfast you'll be if you don't move off from here. My man is an ogre and there's nothing he likes better than boys broiled on toast. You'd better be moving on or he'll soon be coming."

"Oh! please mum, do give me something to eat, mum. I've had nothing to eat since yesterday morning, really and truly, mum," says Jack. "I may as well be broiled as die of hunger."

Well, the ogre's wife was not half so bad after all. So she took Jack into the kitchen and gave him a chunk of bread and cheese and a jug of milk. But Jack hadn't half finished these when thump! thump! thump! the whole house began to tremble with the noise of someone coming.

147

Would you climb a beanstalk that reached to the sky? Why do you think Jack does?

Why doesn't Jack stop and think before he jumps onto the beanstalk?

Why isn't Jack afraid to climb all the way to the sky?

Sample Curriculum Units

···

So the ogre sat down to the breakfast and ate it, but every now and then he would mutter: "Well, I could have sworn—" and he'd get up and search the <u>larder</u> and the cupboards, and everything, only luckily he didn't think of the copper.

After breakfast was over, the ogre called out: "Wife, wife, bring me my golden harp." So she brought it and put it on the table before him. Then he said "Sing!" and the golden harp sang most beautifully. And it went on singing till the ogre fell asleep and commenced to snore like thunder.

Then Jack lifted up the copper lid very quietly and got down like a mouse and crept on hands and knees till he came to the table, when up he crawled, caught hold of the golden harp, and dashed with it towards the door. But the harp called out quite loud "Master! Master!" and the ogre woke up just in time to see Jack running off with his harp.

Would you keep the harp even after it woke up the ogre? Why do you think Jack does?

156

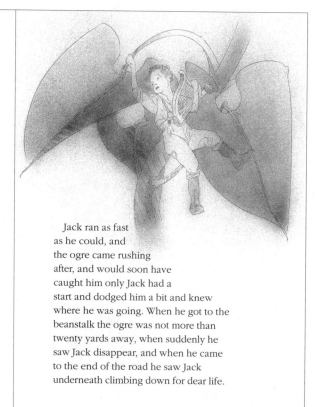

Jack ran as fast as he could, and the ogre came rushing after, and would soon have caught him only Jack had a start and dodged him a bit and knew where he was going. When he got to the beanstalk the ogre was not more than twenty yards away, when suddenly he saw Jack disappear, and when he came to the end of the road he saw Jack underneath climbing down for dear life.

157

Would you keep the harp even after it woke up the ogre? Why do you think Jack does?

Why does Jack endanger himself by keeping hold of the harp after the ogre wakes up?

Why doesn't the harp want to go with Jack?

larder: a place where food is stored

A GAME OF CATCH

Richard Wilbur

SESSION 1

Text Opener: students play the Copy-Cat Game and discuss their reactions to it.

First Reading

Sharing Questions

SESSION 2

Second Reading with Directed Notes: students mark places where they sympathize with a character, and places where they do not sympathize with a character.

SESSION 3

Interpreting Words: students think about why Scho's feelings are so mixed— *self-delighted, intense, exuberant,* and *panicky*—while he is playing his game.

SESSION 4

Shared Inquiry Discussion: students complete the Building Your Answer page; while half the class participates in discussion, the other half reads independently.

Optional Activities: students prepare a passage for textual analysis; students choose a question from the JGB bulletin board and write their answers.

SESSION 5

Creative Writing: students write a story featuring a character who has mixed feelings about a new situation.

Evaluative Writing: students answer the question *Is there any way to be friends with a person like Scho?*

Text Opener

OBJECTIVE

To prepare students to think about how Scho uses his "game" to exert power over Glennie and Monk. To prepare students to think about why the boys are so affected by Scho's verbal game.

Introduce the activity by telling students that they are going to read a story in which one character plays an irritating game with two others. In the Text Opener, students will be playing the Copy-Cat Game and then discussing what kinds of feelings such a game evokes.

Have the class count off and form groups of three. Tell students that, in each group, person #1 will be the Talker, person #2 will be the Imitator, and person #3 will be the Audience.

In the Copy-Cat Game, the Imitator repeats or mimics everything the Talker says or does. For example, if the Talker says, "Let's start," the Imitator says, "Let's start." Or if the Talker says, "I don't want to play anymore," the Imitator says this, too. The Audience watches but does not say or do anything.

Let students play the game for two or three minutes, or until you sense that they have had enough. Then ask the class to take a few minutes to write answers to the appropriate questions on the activity page.

Conclude the activity by having students discuss the final three questions on the activity page. During this discussion, encourage students to refer to the responses they recorded earlier.

Text Opener   A GAME OF CATCH

Name: _____

If you were the **Talker,** answer these questions:
How did it feel to have everything you said repeated?
What did it make you feel like doing?

_____

_____

If you were the **Imitator,** answer these questions:
How did it feel to be the one who did the repeating?
Was it hard to stop playing this game? Why or why not?

_____

_____

If you were the **Audience,** answer these questions:
How did you feel when watching this game? What's the best way to get the one who is doing the repeating to stop?

_____

_____

Now discuss these questions with your class:

What was fun about playing the Copy-Cat Game?

What was disturbing about the Copy-Cat Game?

Why might a person start playing the Copy-Cat Game with someone else?

3

Directed Notes   A GAME OF CATCH

Name:

During your second reading of the story, you marked places where you **sympathize** with a character, and places where you **do not sympathize** with a character.

Now look over your notes and explain whom you sympathize with the most and why.

I sympathize the most with _____ because

1. _____

_____

_____

_____

2. _____

_____

_____

_____

4

OBJECTIVE

To help students think about why Scho plays his game. To help students think about how the characters' different personalities create and intensify their conflict.

Begin the session by writing on the board:

S = I **sympathize** with a character

DS = I do not **sympathize** with a character

Introduce the activity by telling students that their interpretation of the conflict in the story will depend a great deal upon how they feel about the characters. In the Directed Notes activity, students will be thinking about why they respond as they do to Scho, Glennie, and Monk.

Explain to students that sympathize means more than "to feel sorry for"; it also means to understand or side with another person's point of view.

If you want to simplify the activity, have part of the class focus their note taking on Scho and the rest of the class focus on Monk and Glennie.

Follow the usual routine for conducting Directed Notes. As students share their responses, encourage them to elaborate on their thinking by asking *Why do you sympathize with this character here?* and *Why don't you sympathize with this character here?*

After the second reading, students can complete their activity pages in class or as homework.

A GAME OF CATCH

Sample Curriculum
Units

Directed Notes

PAGE 2

Glennie asks Scho, "Got your glove?"

- **S** Is being friendly; tries to find a nice way to tell Scho why they haven't invited him to play
- **DS** Is backhandedly telling Scho that he's not welcome in their game

Scho says, "You could give me some easy grounders, . . . But don't burn 'em."

- **S** Wants to play and knows that this is the only way he can participate; wants to make it easy for the boys to include him
- **DS** Doesn't care that he's asking the boys to make their game more boring; spoils the boys' fun by not letting them continue to pretend they're in the big leagues; disrupts the boys' harmonious teamwork

Monk begins to throw balls to Glennie "once or twice" before letting Scho "have his grounder," and finally gives Scho "a fast, bumpy grounder."

- **S** Is tired of playing the babyish game of throwing simple grounders—wants to "burn" a few balls; is justifiably mad at Scho for butting into the game
- **DS** Is excluding Scho; acts mean by throwing the kind of ball that Scho has said he can't catch

Scho has to chase Monk's ball, makes a bad throw, and finally carries the ball "back to his former position on the lawn," where he "threw it carefully to Glennie."

- **S** Feels hurt because Monk tried to make him look bad; is embarrassed at having to walk the ball back and not being able to throw it

PAGE 3

Glennie suggests to Scho, "Why don't Monk and I catch for five minutes more, and then you can borrow one of our gloves?"

- **S** Tries to be nice to Scho; looks for a way to include Scho that won't make Monk feel cheated; suggests a fair compromise
- **DS** Suggests that Scho drop out of the game; lets Scho know that he's spoiling the game by not having a glove; doesn't plan to keep his promise

Monk tells Scho, "One minute to go," with "a fraction of a grin."

- **DS** Puts Scho off when it's his turn to play; taunts and makes fun of Scho; rubs it in that he controls when Scho will play

Scho watches Glennie and Monk play "for several minutes more."

- **S** Tries to be a good sport, even though he's being treated badly by the boys; probably feels left out and inadequate
- **DS** Should have the sense to know that he's not wanted, and go away

PAGES 3–4

Scho finds "a dangerous chair" in the tree and yells, "I found a wonderful seat up here, . . . If I don't fall out"; he jounces on the branches and sings "in an exaggerated way."

- **S** Tries to get the boys' attention and approval; wants to appear daring; doesn't let the boys get away with ignoring him
- **DS** Wants to make the boys feel guilty and responsible for his peril; stupidly risks his life by jouncing around; acts like an annoying baby; wants to wreck the boys' game if he can't join in

PAGE 4

Scho calls out from the tree, "Do you know what, Monk? . . . I can make you two guys do anything I want."

- **S** Wants to save face by getting back at the boys for treating him badly; finds a clever way to turn the tables and feel important; doesn't want the boys to think that he's a wimp
- **DS** Tries to make Glennie and Monk feel self-conscious and ridiculous; can't be happy unless he's bothering someone

Monk denies that Scho is controlling his actions.

- **S** Feels it's unfair for Scho to wreck their game
- **DS** Lets a silly kid game rattle him unnecessarily; is stupidly falling into Scho's trap

Glennie and **Monk** quit playing catch.

- **S** Have had their game spoiled
- **DS** Should ignore Scho and keep playing; should just leave; should tell Scho that he's bothering them, rather than just wait for him to stop

PAGE 5

Glennie calls up to Scho, "Stop being a dope and come down and we'll play catch for a few minutes."

- **S** Wants to make up with Scho; tries to fix the situation for everyone
- **DS** Doesn't actually apologize to Scho; makes only a grudging offer to include Scho briefly; talks down to Scho

SAMPLE RESPONSES (continued)

PAGE 5 (continued)

Scho hesitates before answering Glennie, in a "tentatively mocking" way, "That's what I wanted you to say."

S	DS
Feels his pride is at stake—part of him wants to stop, but he still needs to prove himself the winner; can't find a face-saving way out of the situation he has created	Rejects Glennie's attempt to make peace; throws away the chance to be a part of the game; continues to be irritating; is stubborn

PAGES 5-6

Monk scrambles awkwardly up the tree, his face "furious and foolish" as he keeps telling Scho to "shut up."

S	DS
Needs to defy the claim that he is being controlled by Scho; feels frustrated at Scho's refusal to respond like a reasonable person; is angry at Scho's unwarranted interference with their serene game	Lets Scho get to him; is out of control—acts in anger and becomes a clumsy fool; should realize that he's making Scho panic

PAGE 6

Monk threatens to "shake the cradle of slight branches in which Scho was sitting."

S	DS
Needs to break the deadlock once and for all	Becomes violent—is going too far by threatening to hurt Scho

PAGE 6 (continued)

Scho falls out of the tree, landing "with a deep thud."

S	DS
Has a painful and frightening experience; doesn't deserve to be physically hurt, no matter how obnoxious he's been	Goes too far—hurts himself in order to hurt Monk

Monk climbs down "crying that honestly he hadn't even touched him, the crazy guy just let go."

S	DS
Is frightened at the thought that he is responsible for Scho's fall; worries that he will be blamed for losing his temper with Scho; feels guilty that he caused Scho's crazy behavior; is concerned that Scho might be seriously hurt	Tries to shirk responsibility

Monk says, "I'm sorry, Scho, . . . I didn't mean to make you fall."

S
Admits his share of the blame for the accident; shows compassion and concern; is no longer angry—is able to set aside the power struggle

PAGE 6 (continued)

Scho tells Monk, "I meant—you to do it. You—had to. You can't do—anything—unless I want—you to."

S	DS
Has to do something to save face; shows some spunk in continuing the game, even though he can barely talk	Can't accept Monk's sincere apology; would rather continue the conflict than reconcile; cares only about winning the power struggle; throws away any chance of having a friendship with Glennie and Monk

Glennie and **Monk** look "helplessly" at Scho and walk away.

S	DS
Feel rejected; understand that there is nothing more they can do for Scho; let Scho "win" his game by leaving	Should have put their feelings aside and helped Scho get home

PAGE 7

Scho croaks "in triumph and misery, 'I want you to do whatever you're going to do for the whole rest of your life!'"

S	DS
Is alone and doesn't know how to be in a friendship; knows that what he's done isn't going to make him happy in the long run; has succeeded in controlling the boys and making them play his game; has found a way to feel superior to the more athletic boys	Is pathetic in his desperate attempt to turn the situation into a victory; is spiteful in not letting the competition end

A GAME OF CATCH

Interpreting Words

OBJECTIVE

To help students think about why Scho has conflicting feelings about his game. To help students think about the extent to which Scho loses control of his own game.

Introduce the session by telling students that, in the Interpreting Words activity, they will be thinking about some of the adjectives the author uses to convey Scho's complicated feelings.

Go over the activity page with the class. Students can answer the first four questions in writing before sharing answers, or they can discuss them as a class. You can also have students work on these questions in pairs or small groups.

Then have students write their responses to the interpretive question *Why does Scho's game give him mixed feelings?*

SAMPLE RESPONSES

Why does Scho's game make him feel **so pleased with himself**?

Is glad to make the boys unhappy, since they made him unhappy; has gotten his way—if he can't play catch, he has made sure the boys can't either; enjoys being up high, looking down on the boys; has proved to the more athletic boys that he can do something hard and daring

What could Scho be thinking that makes him look **intense**?

That he's so clever to have gotten revenge by gaining "power" over the boys; that he's got to figure out what the boys are thinking so that he can decide what to do next; that he's going to make the boys admit that he is smarter and better than they are; that he wants the boys to feel as stupid as they made him feel

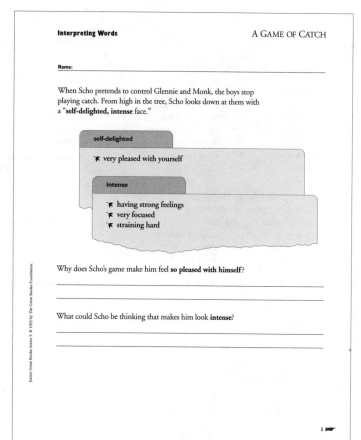

Interpreting Words

A GAME OF CATCH

Name: _____

When Scho pretends to control Glennie and Monk, the boys stop playing catch. From high in the tree, Scho looks down at them with a "**self-delighted, intense** face."

self-delighted
- very pleased with yourself

intense
- having strong feelings
- very focused
- straining hard

Why does Scho's game make him feel **so pleased with himself**?
_____
_____

What could Scho be thinking that makes him look **intense**?
_____
_____

Building Your Answer in Shared Inquiry Discussion

Name: _____

Story Title: _____

Part 1

Your leader's question:

_____

_____

_____

_____

Your answer before discussion:

_____

_____

_____

_____

Junior Great Books Series 5. © 1992 by The Great Books Foundation.

Part 2

After discussion, did you keep the same answer or change your mind?

Your answer after discussion:

_____

_____

_____

_____

_____

What places in the story helped you decide on this answer?

1. _____

_____

_____

_____

_____

2. _____

A GAME OF CATCH

Creative Writing

OBJECTIVE

To help students think further about how Scho's conflicting feelings influence his actions.

Go over the activity page with the class. To clarify the assignment and to help students get ideas for their essays, have a few volunteers suggest some conflicting feelings that a person might have when confronting a new situation, such as being the first girl on an all-boy sports team. You might want to have students expand upon their examples by answering the guiding questions on the activity page.

Creative Writing   A GAME OF CATCH

Name: _____

Scho experiences feelings that are often in conflict with one another.

Write a story about someone who meets a new situation with mixed feelings. Choose one or two of the "positive feelings" and one or two of the "negative feelings" from the lists below to help you create your character's personality.

Positive Feelings

exuberant   hopeful

brave   confident

friendly

Negative Feelings

depressed   panicky

uptight

furious

worried

What is the new situation that your character must face?

_____
_____
_____
_____
_____
_____

Why does this situation cause mixed feelings?

_____
_____
_____

6

Junior Great Books Series 5. © 1993 by The Great Books Foundation.

Creative Writing (continued)   A GAME OF CATCH

_____

_____

_____

_____

How
does your
character handle
the situation?
Which feelings
win out?

_____

_____

_____

_____

_____

_____

_____

_____

_____

Does your
character end
up in triumph,
misery, or
both?

_____

_____

_____

_____

_____

_____

_____

_____

A GAME OF CATCH

Evaluative Writing

OBJECTIVE

To help students think further about the extent to which they believe Scho is responsible for his own loneliness and unhappiness.

See the explanation on the activity page.

Evaluative Writing   A GAME OF CATCH

Name: _____

Glennie and Monk are unable to reach an understanding with Scho.

Write an essay answering this question:
Is there any way to be friends with a person like Scho?

Do you see any good qualities in Scho that would make being his friend worthwhile?

What would be the hardest thing about being friends with Scho?

Evaluative Writing (continued)

How would you build on Scho's good qualities or try to change his bad qualities?

Do you think you could succeed in being friends with Scho?

The Melian Dialogue
Thucydides

Prereading Questions

1. Which is more important—freedom or survival?

2. How can hope sometimes give you strength, and sometimes mislead you?

3. Is it honorable or stupid to carry on a fight against overwhelming odds? Is honor more important than life itself?

4. Can a slave live a dignified and honorable life?

5. Why is it sometimes hard to remain neutral in an argument or fight? Do you respect people who try not to take sides in a dispute?

Interpretive Note Source (first or second reading)

Mark places where you think the Athenians give a good reason for the Melians to surrender. Mark places where you think the Melians give a good reason for refusing to surrender.

Interpretive Questions for Discussion

1. Are the Melians fools or heroes for refusing the Athenian offer?

2. Do the Melians have a keener sense of honor than the Athenians do, or are they merely using honor as a ploy for getting out of a tight spot?

3. Do the Athenians have a bad conscience about attacking the Melians?

4. Are the Melians or the Athenians more responsible for the fate of the Melians?

5. Why do the Athenians think they will fare better if their subjects fear them than if their subjects trust them?

6. Why do the Athenians give the Melians a chance to avoid a battle? Why do they try to convince the Melians that might makes right, rather than just threatening them with their power?

7. Why do the Athenians assume that a show of generosity and friendship towards the Melians would be a sign of weakness rather than of confidence?

8. Do the Athenians believe that they are treating the Melians, their "inferiors," fairly? (31)

9. Why do the Athenians not merely subdue the Melians, but wipe them out altogether?

10. Why do the Melians think it would be "criminal cowardice" to submit to the great strength of the Athenians? (28)

11. Why do the Melians put so much trust in the Lacedaemonian "sense of honor"? (29)

12. Why are we told that it is treachery from within, rather than Athenian power, that eventually subdues the Melians? (33)

13. Why does Thucydides tell us that the Lacedaemonians turned back from assisting Melos because they "found the sacrifices for crossing unfavorable"? (33)

14. Why do the Athenians make clear from the beginning that they do not want to speak of justice?

15. Are we meant to think the Athenians are barbaric, or just trying to survive in a hard, dog-eat-dog world?

Passages for Textual Analysis

Pages 26-27: beginning, "ATHENIANS: Then we will not make a long and unconvincing speech," and ending, "involve you in a crushing punishment that would be a lesson to the world."

Pages 29-30: beginning, "ATHENIANS: Hope encourages men to take risks," and ending, "and danger is a risk which the Lacedaemonians are little inclined to run."

Page 31: beginning, "ATHENIANS: Here experience may teach you like others," and ending, "and that its prosperity or ruin depends on one decision."

Post-Discussion Writing

1. Should the Melians have surrendered to the Athenians?

2. Were the Athenians justified in destroying the Melians, after giving them the option of surrender?

3. Is belief in pacifism and nonviolence an impractical attitude in a dangerous world?

4. Is it better to be idealistic or pragmatic?

5. Are the Melian rulers poor leaders? If you were one of the Melian people, what would you say to your leaders on finding out they had refused the Athenian offer?

6. Does the "natural law" that the strong always rule over the weak apply to a democracy? (29)

7. What might countries facing Nazi Germany in World War II have learned from "The Melian Dialogue"?